WESTERN AMERICAN LITERATURE:

A Bibliography of Interpretive Books and Articles

by

Richard W. Etulain
Idaho State University

Dakota Press
1972

University of South Dakota, Vermillion, S.D. 57069

For
Marian Washburn
and
Bob Woodward

Two Easterners Who Came West

PREFACE

The following bibliography is intended as a handy checklist for students and scholars interested in Western American literature. Although the listing is not exhaustive, it is comprehensive and brings together in one volume for the first time the most important research on the literature of the American West. I have stressed recent work and have included material published through 1971.

The checklist is divided into five major sections: (1) bibliographies listing research on western American literature; (2) anthologies of western literature; (3) general works, which are divided into two categories: (a) books, theses, and disserations and (b) articles; (4) listings of research dealing with three important topics of western American literature: (a) the Beats, (b) local color and regionalism, and (c) the Western, which contains items on the formula Western and western movies; and (5) works on individual authors. There is some overlapping among the sections because some items discuss more than one subject.

The bibliography lists primarily the research on authors who were born and reared in the trans-Mississippi West or who have spent significant portions of their lives in the region. Yet I have also included items on writers like James Fenimore Cooper, Stephen Crane, Nathaniel West, and Thomas Berger whose works have a significant impact on western literature. Major emphasis is placed on writers of fiction and poetry, but some books and articles dealing with writers of non-fiction have also been included.

Those readers interested in additional listings of research ought to follow closely the yearly bibliographies appearing in Winter issues of *Western American Literature*. Also helpful are the listings in the yearly *MLA International Bibliography*, the lists in each issue of American Literature, and the checklists that appear in *Western Historical Quarterly*.

For aid in preparing this bibliography, I wish to thank the staff of the Idaho State University Library, Dean Joseph Hearst for securing financial help in times of tightening budgets, and Marcie Bell for gathering obscure items. Most of all, I wish to thank Laura Hunt who cheerfully and most competently helped me at every stage in putting together this project.

I invite suggestions for corrections and additions to future editions of the bibliography.

CONTENTS

xi

BIBLIOGRAPHIES

Adams, Ramon F. *Burs under the Saddle: A Second Look at Books and Histories of the West.* Norman: University of Oklahoma Press, 1964.

Adams, Ramon F. *The Rampaging Herd: A Bibliography of Books and Pamphlets on Men and Events in the Cattle Industry.* Norman: University of Oklahoma Press, 1959.

Adams, Ramon F. *Six-Guns and Saddle Leather: A Bibliography of Books and Pamphlets on Western Outlaws and Gunmen.* Norman: University of Oklahoma Press, 1954, 1969.

American Literature. 1929—. Each issue contains a checklist of current articles and a listing of dissertations in progress or completed.

American Quarterly. (1949—). An annual bibliography of American Studies is issued.

Bay, Jens C. *A Handful of Western Books.* Cedar Rapids, Iowa, 1935.

Bay, Jens C. *A Second Handful of Western Books.* Cedar Rapids, Iowa, 1936.

Bay, Jens C. *A Third Handful of Western Books.* Cedar Rapids, Iowa, 1937.

Bay, Jens C. "Western Life and Western Books." *Missouri Historical Review*, XXXVI (1942), 403-11.

Bragin, Charles. *Dime Novels: Bibliography, 1860-1928.* Brooklyn, 1938.

Bryer, Jackson R., ed. *Fifteen Modern American Authors: A Survey of Research and Criticism.* Durham: Duke University Press, 1969. Contains sections on Cather and Steinbeck.

Bullen, John S., ed. "Annual Bibliography of Studies in Western American Literature." *Western American Literature.* Issued each year in the Winter issue.

Carson, W. G. B. "The Theatre of the American Frontier: A Bibliography." *Theatre Research*, I (March 1958), 14-23.

Coan, Otis W., and Richard G. Lillard. *America in Fiction, an Annotated List of Novels that Interpret Aspects of Life in the U.S.* 4th ed. Stanford, California, 1956.

Cole, Wendell. "Early Theatre West of the Rockies: A Bibliographical Essay." *Theatre Research*, IV (1962), 36-45.

Coleman, Rufus A., general editor. *Northwest Books: First Supplement.* Lincoln: University of Nebraska Press, 1949.

Davidson, Levette J. *Rocky Mountain Life in Literature: a Descriptive Bibliography.* Denver: University of Denver Book Store, 1936.

Dobie, J. Frank. *Guide to Life and Literature of the Southwest*. Rev. ed. Dallas: Southern Methodist University Press, 1952.

Dondore, Dorothy Anne. *The Prairie and the Making of Middle America: Four Centuries of Description*. Cedar Rapids, Iowa: The Torch Press, 1926.

Dougherty, Charles T. "Novels of the Middle Border: A Critical Bibliography for Historians." *Historical Bulletin*, XXV (May 1947), 77-8, 85-8.

Flanagan, John T. "A Bibliography of Middle Western Farm Novels." *Minnesota History*, XXIII (June 1942), 156-8.

Gaston, Edwin W., Jr. *The Early Novel of the Southwest*. Albuquerque: University of New Mexico Press, 1961, 195-302.

Gerstenberger, Donna and George Hendrick. *The American Novel 1789-1959: A Checklist of Twentieth-Century Criticism*. Denver: Alan Swallow, 1961.

Gerstenberger, Donna, and George Hendrick. *The American Novel: A Checklist of Twentieth Century Criticism on Novels Since 1789. Volume II: Criticism Written 1960-1968*. Chicago: Swallow Press, 1970.

Gohdes, Clarence. *Bibliographical Guide to the Study of Literature of the U.S.A.* Third edition, revised and enlarged. Durham: Duke University Press, 1970.

Gohdes, Clarence. *Literature and Theatre of the States and Regions of the U.S.A.: An Historical Bibliography*. Durham: Duke University Press, 1967. Excellent listing for each western state and other lists for the Western and regionalism. Very useful.

Griffith, Doris, *et al.* "A Regional Bibliography." *Western Humanities Review*, VI (1952), 207-12.

Hill, Gertrude. "The Southwest in Verse: A Selective Bibliography of Arizona and New Mexican Poetry." *Arizona Quarterly*, XXIII (1967), 306-12.

Jones, Howard Mumford, and Richard M. Ludwig. *Guide to American Literature and Its Backgrounds since 1890*. 3rd Edition, Revised and Enlarged. Cambridge: Harvard University Press, 1964.

Kheridian, David. *Six Poets of the San Francisco Renaissance*. Fresno: The Giligia Press, 1967.

Kimball, Richard R. "Beginnings of Literature Based on the American Frontier: Descriptive Bibliography." Unpublished master's thesis, University of Southern California, 1950.

Kurtz, Kenneth. *Literature of the American Southwest: A Selective Bibliography*. Los Angeles, 1956.

Leary, Lewis. *Articles on American Literature 1950-1967*. Durham: Duke University Press, 1970.

Logasa, Hannah. *Regional United States: A Subject List.* Boston, 1942.

Lyon, Thomas J., ed. "Research in Western American Literature." *Western American Literature.* Appears annually in the Winter issue and lists theses and dissertations completed or in progress on Western American literature.

McNamee, Lawrence F. *Dissertations in English and American Literature . . . 1865-1914.* New York: R. R. Bowker, 1968; *Supplement One . . . 1964-1968, 1969.*

McLean, Malcolm. "In the Beginning." *Southwestern American Literature,* I (January 1971), 5-7.

Major, Mabel, Rebecca W. Smith, and T. M. Pearce, eds. *Southwest Heritage.* Albuquerque: University of New Mexico Press, 1938; Rev. ed. 1948.

Meyer, Roy W. "An Annotated Bibliography of Middle Western Farm Fiction, 1891-1962." *The Middle Western Farm Novel in the Twentieth Century.* Lincoln: University of Nebraska Press, 1965, 200-42.

Milton, John R. "Selected Bibliography of Materials Relating to the Western American Novel." *South Dakota Review.* II (Autumn 1964), 101-8; IV (Summer 1966), 79-80.

MLA International Bibliography. Published annually in hard covers and includes a large section on American literature.

Nilon, Charles H. *Bibliography of Bibliographies in American Literature.* New York: R. R. Bowker Company, 1970. The best single source for general bibliographies.

Northwest Books. Portland: Binfords and Mort, 1942.

Pollard, Lancaster. "A Check List of Washington Authors." *Pacific Northwest Quarterly,* XXXI (1940), 3-96; XXXV (1944), 233-66.

Paluka, Frank. *Iowa Authors: A Bio-Bibliography of Sixty Native Writers.* Iowa City: Friends of the University of Iowa Libraries, 1967.

Rubin, Louis D., ed. *A Bibliographical Guide to the Study of Southern Literature.* Baton Rouge: Louisiana State University Press, 1969.

Rundell, Walter, Jr. "Interpretations of the American West: A Descriptive Bibliography." *Arizona and the West,* III (Spring 1961), 69-88; (Summer 1961), 148-68.

Rusk, Ralph Leslie. *The Literature of the Middle Western Frontier.* 2 vols. New York: Columbia University Press, 1925.

Sackett, S. J., compiler. "Master's Theses in Literature." *Lit,* VIII (November 1967), 45-174.

Streeter, Thomas W. "Notes on North American Regional Bibliographies." *Papers of the Bibliographical Society of America,* XXXVI (1942), 171-86.

Van Derhoff, Jakc. *A Bibliography of Novels Related to American Frontier and Colonial History.* Troy, New York: The Whitson Publishing Company, 1971.

Wagner, H. R. *The Plains and the Rockies: A Bibliography of Original Narratives of Travel and Adventure, 1800-1865.* San Francisco, 1921.

West, Ray B. *Writing in the Rocky Mountains with a Bibliography by Nellie Cliff.* Lincoln: University of Nebraska Press, 1947.

Winther, Oscar O. *A Classified Bibliography of the Periodical Literature of the Trans-Mississippi West (1811-1957).* Bloomington: University of Indiana Press, 1961.

Winther, Oscar O. *The Trans-Mississippi West: A Guide to Its Periodical Literature (1811-1938).* Bloomington: University of Indiana Press, 1943.

Woodress, James. *Dissertations in American Literature 1891-1966.* Durham: Duke University Press, 1968.

Woodress, James, ed. *Eight American Authors.* Revised Edition. New York: W. W. Norton, 1972.

ANTHOLOGIES

Babcock, C. Merton. *The American Frontier: A Social and Literary Record.* New York: Holt, Rinehart and Winston, 1965.

Becker, Mary L. *Golden Tales of the Far West.* New York, 1935.

Blacker, Irwin R. *The Old West in Fiction.* New York, 1961.

Botkin, Benjamin Albert, ed. *A Treasury of Western Folklore.* New York: Crown Publishers, 1944.

Brandon, William. *The Magic World: American Indian Songs and Poems.* New York: William Morrow and Company, 1971.

Caughey, John and LaRee, ed. *California Heritage.* Los Angeles: Ward Ritchie Press, 1962; Rev. ed., Itasca, Illinois: F. E. Peacock, 1971.

Coggeshall, William T. *The Poets and Poetry of the West,* 1860.

Coleman, Rufus A. *The Golden West in Story and Verse.* New York, 1941.

Coleman, Rufus A. *Western Prose and Poetry.* New York, 1932.

Cummins, D. Duane, and William Gee White, eds. *The American Frontier.* New York: Benziger Brothers, 1968.

Davidson, Levette J. *Poems of the Old West: A Rocky Mountain Anthology.* Denver, Colorado, 1951.

Davidson, Levette J., and Prudence Bostwick. *The Literature of the Rocky Mountain West, 1803-1903.* Caldwell, Idaho: The Caxton Printers, 1939.

Davidson, Levette J., and Forrester Blake. *Rocky Mountain Tales.* Norman: University of Oklahoma Press, 1947.

Day, A. Grove. *The Sky Clears: Poetry of the American Indians.* Lincoln: University of Nebraska Press, 1964.

Durham, Philip, and Everett L. Jones, ed. *The Frontier in American Literature.* New York: The Odyssey Press, 1969.

Flanagan, John T., ed. *America is West: An Anthology of Middlewestern Life and Literature.* Minneapolis: University of Minnesota Press, 1945.

Frederick, John T., ed. *Out of the Midwest: An Anthology of Midwestern Writing.* New York: Whittlesey House, 1944.

Gallagher, William D. *Selections from the Poetical Literature of the West,* 1841.

Greenberg, David B., compiler. *The Land Our Fathers Plowed.* Norman: University of Oklahoma Press, 1969.

Greenway, John. *Folklore of the Great West.* Palo Alto: The American West Publishing Company, 1969.

Hine, Robert V., and Edwin R. Bingham, eds. *The Frontier Experience: Readings in the Trans-Mississippi West.* Belmont, California: Wadsworth Publishing Company, 1963.

Hoffman, Hans A. *Poets of the Western Scene: Poems from Westward, a National Magazine of Verse.* San Leandro, California, 1937.

Holbrook, Stewart H., ed. *Promised Land: A Collection of Northwest Writing.* New York: Whittlesey House, 1945.

Jackson, Joseph Henry, ed. *Continent's End: A Collection of California Writing.* New York: Whittlesey House, 1944.

Lee, Charles. *North, East, South, West: A Regional Anthology of American Writing.* New York, 1945.

Lee, W. Storrs, ed. *California: A Literary Chronicle.* New York: Funk and Wagnalls, 1969. See also Lee's similar anthology of Colorado writing.

Lee, W. Storrs, ed. *Washington State: A Literary Chronicle.* New York: Funk and Wagnalls, 1969.

Lomax, John A., collector. *Cowboy Songs and Other Frontier Ballads.* New York: The Macmillan Company, 1927.

Lucia, Ellis. *This Land Around Us: A Treasury of Pacific Northwest Writing.* New York: Doubleday and Co., 1969.

Lyons, Richard, ed. *Poetry North.* Fargo: North Dakota Institute for Regional Studies, 1970.

Maule, Harry E., ed. *Great Tales of the American West.* New York: Modern Library, 1945.

Meredith, Scott. *Bar 1: Roundup of Best Western Stories.* New York, 1952.

Meredith, Scott. *Bar 2: Roundup of Best Western Stories.* New York, 1953. Meredith later edited several other anthologies of this type.

Milton, John R., ed. *The American Indian Speaks.* Vermillion: Dakota Press, 1969.

Milton, John R., ed. *American Indian II.* Vermillion: Dakota Press, 1971.

Newman, May W. *Poetry of the Pacific: Selections and Original Poems . . .* San Francisco, California, 1867.

Pearce, Thomas M., and Telfair Hendon, eds. *America in the Southwest: A Regional Anthology.* Albuquerque: The University of New Mexico Press, 1933.

Pearce, T. M., and A. P. Thomason, eds. *Southwesterners Write.* Albuquerque: The University of New Mexico Press, 1947.

Perry, George Sessions, ed. *Roundup Time: A Collection of Southwestern Writing.* New York: Whittlesey House, 1943.

Powell, Lawrence Clark. *California Classics: The Creative Literature of the Golden State.* Los Angeles: Ward Ritchie Press, [1971].

Romano V, Octavio Ignacio, ed. *El Espejo (The Mirror): Selected Mexican-American Literature.* Berkeley: Quinto Sol Publications, 1969.

Schaefer, Jack. *Out West: An Anthology of Stories.* Boston, 1955.

Shockley, Martin, ed. *Southwest Writers Anthology.* Austin, Texas: Steck-Vaughn Company, 1967.

Silber, Irwin. *Songs of the Great American West.* New York: The Macmillan Company, 1967.

Spence, Clark C., ed. *The American West: A Source Book.* New York: Thomas Y. Crowell, 1966.

Sterling, George, *et al. Continent's End.* San Francisco, California, 1925.

Stevens, A. Wilbur, ed. *Poems Southwest.* Prescott, Arizona: Prescott College Press, 1968.

Targ, William. *The American West: A Treasury of Stories, Legends, Narratives, Songs, & Ballads of Western America.* New York and Cleveland: World Publishing Company, 1946.

Targ, William, ed. *Western Story Omnibus.* Cleveland: The World Publishing Company, 1945.

Taylor, J. Golden, ed. *Great Western Short Stories.* Palo Alto: The American West Publishing Company, 1967. Still the best collection available.

Taylor, J. Golden, ed. *The Literature of the American West.* Boston: Houghton Mifflin, 1971. The best anthology of Western American literature.

6

Thorp, N. Howard ("Jack"). *Songs of the Cowboys,* edited by Austin E. and Alta S. Fife. New York: Clarkson N. Potter, Inc., 1966.

Ward, Don, ed. *Great Short Novels of the American West.* New York: Collier Books, 1962.

Ward, Don. *Wild Streets: Tales of the Frontier Towns, by Members of the Western Writers of America.* Garden City, New York, 1958.

West, Ray B., ed. *The Rocky Mountain Reader.* New York: E. P. Dutton & Company, 1946.

A Western Sample: Nine Contemporary Poets. Georgetown, California, 1963.

Winters, Yvor. *Poets of the Pacific, Second Series.* Stanford, California, 1949.

GENERAL WORKS

I. BOOKS

Ahnebrink, Lars. *The Beginnings of Naturalism in American Fiction: A Study of the Works of Hamlin Garland, Stephen Crane, and Frank Norris.* Cambridge: Harvard University Press, 1950.

Alter, Judith. "The Western Myth in American Painting and Fiction of the Late 19th and Early 20th Centuries." Unpublished doctoral dissertation, Texas Christian University, 1970.

Bankston, Darena. "Pioneering on the Plains as Portrayed by American Woman Novelists." Unpublished master's thesis, Texas Christian University, 1966.

Barsness, John A. "The Breaking of the Myth: A Study of the Cultural Implications in the Western Novel in the Twentieth Century." Unpublished doctoral dissertation, University of Minnesota, 1966.

Berthoff, Warner. *The Ferment of Realism: American Literature, 1884-1919.* New York: The Free Press, 1965.

Blaine, Harold A. "The Frontiersman in American Prose and Fiction, 1800-1860." Unpublished doctoral dissertation, Western Reserve University, 1936.

Blair, Walter, and Franklin J. Meine. *Half Horse, Half Alligator: The Growth of the Mike Fink Legend.* Chicago: University of Chicago Press, 1956.

Boatright, Mody C. *Folk Laughter on the American Frontier.* New York: Collier Books, 1961.

Boynton, Percy H. *The Rediscovery of the Frontier*. Chicago: University of Chicago Press, 1931.

Branch, E. Douglas. *The Cowboy and His Interpreters*. New York: D. Appleton and Co., 1926, 1961.

Bridges, Emily. *The Great West: In Fact and Fiction*. University of North Carolina Library Extension Publication, XVIII (January 1953).

Brier, Howard. *Sawdust Empire: The Pacific Northwest*. New York: Alfred A. Knopf, 1958.

Brooks, Van Wyck. *The Confident Years: 1885-1915*. New York: E. P. Dutton, 1952.

Campbell, Walter S. *The Book Lover's Southwest*. Norman, University of Oklahoma Press, 1955.

Chase, Richard. *The American Novel and Its Tradition*. Garden City: Doubleday and Co., 1957.

Chittick, V.L.O., ed. *Northwest Harvest: A Regional Stocktaking*. New York: The Macmillan Company, 1948.

Clifford, John. "Social and Political Attitudes of Fiction of Ranch and Range." Unpublished doctoral dissertation, University of Iowa, 1954.

Clough, Wilson O. *The Necessary Earth*. Austin: University of Texas Press, 1964.

Colquitt, Betsy F. *A Part of Space: Ten Texas Writers*. Fort Worth: Texas Christian University Press, 1969.

Çoon, Gilbert D. "The Easterner in the Western Historical Novel." Unpublished doctoral dissertation, Washington State University, 1970.

Culmsee, Carlton F. *Malign Nature and the Frontier*. Logan, Utah: Utah State University Press, 1959.

De Menil, Alexander Nicholas. *The Literature of the Louisiana Territory*. St. Louis: The St. Lewis News Company, 1904.

Dobie, J. Frank. *Guide to Life and Literature of the Southwest*. Dallas: Southern Methodist University Press, 1943, 1952.

Dondore, Dorothy. *The Prairie and the Making of Middle America*. Cedar Rapids: Torch Press, 1926.

Durham, Philip, and Everett L. Jones. *The Negro Cowboys*. New York: Dodd, Mead, 1965.

Evans, James Leroy. "The Indian Savage, the Mexican Bandit, the Chinese Heathen—Three Popular Stereotypes." Unpublished doctoral dissertation, University of Texas, 1967.

Fielder, Leslie. *The Return of the Vanishing American*. New York: Stein and Day, 1968.

Fenin, George N., and William K. Everson. *The Western: From Silents to Cinerama*. New York: Bonanza Books, 1962.

Fishwick, Marshall. *The American Hero: Myth and Reality.* Washington: Public Affairs Press, 1954.

Fleck, Byron Y. "The West as Viewed by Foreign Travelers, 1783-1840." Unpublished doctoral dissertation, University of Iowa, 1950.

Folsom, James K. *The American Western Novel.* New Haven: College and University Press, 1966.

Fowler, Bill. "The Treatment of Religion in the Humor of the Old Southwest." Unpublished master's thesis, University of Texas, 1966.

Frantz, Joe B., and Julian E. Choate, Jr. *The American Cowboy: The Myth and the Reality.* Norman: University of Oklahoma Press, 1955.

Fussell, Edwin. *Frontier: American Literature and the American West.* Princeton: Princeton University Press, 1965.

Galinski, Hans, ed. *The Frontier in American History and Literature.* Verlag Moritz Diesterweg, 1960.

Gard, Wayne. *Reminiscenses of Range Life.* Southwest Writers Series, No. 30. Austin, Texas: Steck-Vaughn Company, 1970.

Gaston, Edwin W., Jr. *The Early Novel of the Southwest.* Albuquerque: The University of New Mexico Press, 1961.

Hairston, Joel Beck. "The Westerner's Dilemma: A Study of Modern Western Fiction." Unpublished doctoral dissertation, University of Minnesota, 1970.

Harkness, David James. *The Literary Midwest.* University of Tennessee News Letter, XXXVII (February 1958).

Harkness, David James. *Literary Trails of the Western States.* University of Tennessee News Letter, XXXIV (July 1955).

Harkness, David James. *The Southwest and West Coast in Literature.* The University of Tennessee News Letter, XXXIII (October 1954).

Haslam, Gerald. *Forgotten Pages of American Literature.* New York: Houghton Mifflin, 1970.

Hazard, Lucy Lockwood. *The Frontier in American Literature.* New York: Thomas Y. Crowell Co., 1927, 1941, 1960.

Herron, Ima Honaker. *The Small Town in American Literature.* Durham: Duke University Press, 1939.

Hilfer, Anthony Channell. *The Revolt from the Village, 1915-1930.* Chapel Hill: University of North Carolina Press, 1969.

Hodgins, Francis E., Jr. "The Literary Emancipation of a Region: The Changing Image of the American West in Fiction." Unpublished doctoral dissertation, Michigan State University, 1957.

Howard, Richard. *Alone with America: Essays on the Art of Poetry in the United States.* New York: Atheneum, 1969.

Hubbell, Jay B. *South and Southwest: Literary Essays and Reminiscences.* Durham: Duke University Press, 1965.

Hudson, Ruth, *et al. Studies in Literature of the West: University of Wyoming Publications.* Laramie: University of Wyoming, 1956.

Jacobson, Harvey K. "A Study of Novels About North Dakota." Unpublished master's thesis, University of North Dakota, 1956.

Johannsen, Albert. *The House of Beadle and Adams and Its Dime and Nickel Novels.* Norman: University of Oklahoma Press, 1950; Supplement, 1962.

Jones, Howard Mumford. *The Frontier in American Fiction: Four Lectures on the Relation of Landscape to Literature.* Jerusalem: Magness Press, Hebrew University, 1956.

Jones, Joel M. "Everyman's Usable Past: The American Historical Novel." Unpublished doctoral dissertation, University of New Mexico, 1966.

Karolides, Nicholas J. *The Pioneer in the American Novel: 1900-1950.* Norman: University of Oklahoma Press, 1967.

Kay, Arthur M. "The Epic Intent and the American Dream: The Westering Theme in Modern American Poetry." Unpublished doctoral dissertation, Columbia University, 1961.

Keiser, Albert. *The Indian in American Literature.* New York: Oxford University Press, 1933.

Kennedy, Sister Patricia. "The Pioneer Woman in Middle Western Fiction." Unpublished doctoral dissertation, University of Illinois, 1968.

Kites, Jim. *Horizons West: Studies in Authorship in the Western Film.* Bloomington: Indiana University Press, 1970.

Leach, Joseph. *The Typical Texan: Biography of an American Myth.* Dallas: Southern Methodist University Press, 1952.

Lee, Robert Edson. *From West to East: Studies in The Literature of the American West.* Urbana: University of Illinois Press, 1966.

Leisy, Ernest E. *The American Historical Novel.* Norman: University of Oklahoma Press, 1950.

Lewis, Merrill E. "American Frontier History as Literature: Studies in Historiography of George Bancroft, Frederick Jackson Turner, and Theodore Roosevelt." Unpublished doctoral dissertation, University of Utah, 1968.

Lyon, Peter. *The Wild Wild West.* New York: Funk and Wagnalls, 1969.

McDermott, John Francis, ed. *Travelers on the Western Frontier.* Urbana: University of Illinois Press, 1970.

McMurtry, Larry. *In a Narrow Grave: Essays on Texas.* Austin: The Encino Press, 1968.

Marovitz, Sanford E. "Frontier Conflicts, Villains, Outlaws, and Indians in Selected Western Fiction, 1799-1860." Unpublished doctoral dissertation, Duke University, 1968.

Martin, Jay. *Harvests of Change: American Literature 1865-1914.* Englewood Cliffs, N.J.: Prentice-Hall, 1967.

Meyer, Roy W. *The Middle Western Farm Novel in the Twentieth Century.* Lincoln: University of Nebraska Press, 1965.

Miles, Elton. *Southwest Humorists.* Southwest Writers Series, No. 26. Austin, Texas: Steck-Vaughn Company, 1969.

Morgan, H. Wayne. *American Writers in Rebellion from Twain to Dreiser.* New York: Hill and Wang, 1965. Deals with Twain, Norris, Garland.

Morgan, Paul. "The Treatment of the Indian in Southwestern Literature since 1915: A Study in Primitivism." Unpublished doctoral dissertation, University of Texas, 1954.

Morris, Wright. *The Territory Ahead.* New York: Harcourt, 1958.

Nash, Roderick. *Wilderness and the American Mind.* New Haven: Yale University Press, 1967.

Nelson, Herbert B. *The Literary Impulse in Pioneer Oregon.* Corvallis: Oregon State College Press, 1948.

Noble, David. *The Eternal Adam and the New World Garden: The Central Myth in the American Novel Since 1830.* New York: George Brazilier, 1968.

Noel, Mary. *Villains Galore . . . the Heyday of the Popular Story Weekly.* New York: The Macmillan Company, 1954.

Pearce, Roy Harvey. *The Savages of America: A Study of the Indian and the Idea of Civilization.* Baltimore: The Johns Hopkins Press, 1953.

Peterson, Levi. "The Ambivalence of Alienation: The Debate Over the Frontier Freedom in the Quality Western Novel of the Twentieth Century." Unpublished doctoral dissertation, University of Utah, 1965.

Pizer, Donald. *Realism and Naturalism in 19th Century American Literature.* Carbondale: Southern Illinois University Press, 1966.

Powers, Alfred. *History of Oregon Literature.* Portland: Metropolitan Press, 1935.

Prose and Poetry of the Livestock Industry of the United States. Denver: National Live Stock Historical Association, 1905.

Robinson, Cecil. *With the Ears of Strangers: The Mexican in American Literature.* Tucson: University of Arizona Press, 1963.

Rodgers, John William. *Finding Literature on the Texas Plains.* Dallas: The Southwest Press, 1931.

Rosa, Joseph G. *The Gunfighter: Man or Myth.* Norman: University of Oklahoma Press, 1969.

11

Rusk, Ralph Leslie. *The Literature of the Middle Western Frontier.* 2 vols. New York: Columbia University Press, 1925.

Schmitt, Peter J. *Back to Nature: The Arcadian Myth in Urban America.* New York: Oxford University Press, 1969.

See, Carolyn P. "The Hollywood Novel: An Historical and Critical Study." Unpublished doctoral dissertation, University of California at Los Angeles, 1963.

Shames, Priscilla. "The Treatment of the American Indian in Western American Fiction." Unpublished doctoral dissertation, University of California at Los Angeles, 1970.

Simonson, Harold P. *The Closed Frontier: Studies in American Literary Tragedy.* New York: Holt, Rinehart and Winston, Inc., 1970.

Smith, Henry Nash. *Virgin Land: The American West as Symbol and Myth.* Cambridge: Harvard University Press, 1950, 1970.

Sonnichsen, C. L. *Cowboys and Cattle Kings.* Norman, University of Oklahoma Press, 1950.

Steckmesser, Kent L. *The Western Hero in History and Legend.* Norman: University of Oklahoma Press, 1965.

Stegner, Wallace. *The Sound of Mountain Water.* New York: Doubleday and Company, Inc., 1969.

Sutton, Ann and Myron. *The American West: A Natural History.* New York: Random House, 1970.

Taft, Robert. *Artists and Illustrators of the Old West.* New York: Scribners, 1953.

Tebbel, John. *Fact and Fiction Problems of the Historical Novelist.* Lansing: Historical Society of Michigan, 1962.

Tinker, Edward Larocque. *The Horsemen of the Americas and the Literature They Inspired.* Austin: University of Texas Press, 1967.

Todd, Edgeley W. "Literary Interest in the Fur Trade and Fur Trapper of the Trans-Mississippi West." Unpublished doctoral dissertation, Northwestern University, 1952.

Venable, William H. *Beginnings of Literary Culture in the Ohio Valley.* Cincinnati: Robert Clarke and Co., 1891.

Walker, Franklin. *A Literary History of Southern California.* Berkeley: University of California Press, 1950.

Walker, Franklin. *San Francisco's Literary Frontier.* New York: Knopf, 1939; Seattle: University of Washington Press, 1969.

Walker, Franklin. *The Seacoast of Bohemia: An Account of Early Carmel.* San Francisco: The Book Club of California, 1966.

Walker, Robert H. *The Poet and the Gilded Age.* Philadelphia: University of Pennsylvania Press, 1963.

Webb, Walter P. *The Great Plains.* Boston, 1931; New York, 1957.

Weber, Harley R. "Midwestern Farm Writing in the Late Nineteenth Century: A Study in Changing Attitudes." Unpublished doctoral dissertation, University of Minnesota, 1968.

Wecter, Dixon. *The Hero in America.* New York: Charles Scribner's Sons, 1941.

Le Western: Sources, Thèmes, mythologies, auteurs, acteurs, filmographies. Paris: Union Général d' Editions, 1966.

White, G. Edward. *The Eastern Establishment and the Western Experience.* New Haven: Yale University Press, 1968.

Wilson, Edmund. *The Boys in the Backroom: Notes on California Novelists.* San Francisco, 1941.

Wyman, Walker D., and Clifton B. Kroeber, eds. *The Frontier in Perspective.* Madison: University of Wisconsin Press, 1957.

Ziff, Larzer. *The American 1890s: Life and Times of a Lost Gerneration.* New York: The Viking Press, 1966.

II. ARTICLES

Adams, Andy. "Western Interpreters." *Southwest Review,* X (October 1924), 70-4.

Anderson, John Q. "Scholarship in Southwestern Humor: Past and Present." *Mississippi Quarterly,* XVII (1964), 67-86.

Arrington, Leonard J. and Jon Haupt. "Intolerable Zion: The Image of Mormonism in Nineteenth Century American Literature." *Western Humanities Review,* XXII (Summer 1968), 243-60.

Athearn, Robert G. *High Country Empire: The High Plains and Rockies.* New York: McGraw-Hill, 1960. Includes a chapter on the literature of the area.

Atherton, L. E. "The Midwestern Country Town—Myth and Reality." *Agricultural History,* XXVI (July 1952), 73-80.

Attebery, Louie. "The American West and the Archetypal Orphan." *Western American Literature,* V (Fall 1970), 205-17.

Autor, Hans. "Alaskan Poetry." *Alaska Review,* I (Spring 1964), 48-55.

Baker, Joseph E. "Four Arguments for Regionalism." *Saturday Review,* XV (November 28, 1936), 3-4, 14.

Baker, Joseph E. "Regionalism in the Middle West." *American Review,* IV (March 1935), 604-14.

Banks, Loy Otis. "The Credible Literary West." *Colorado Quarterly,* VIII (Summer 1959), 28-50.

Baritz, Loren. "The Idea of the West." *American Historical Review,* XLVI (April 1969), 618-40.

Barker, Warren J. "The Stereotyped Western Story." *Psychoanalytic Quarterly,* XXIV (June 1955), 270-280.

Barsness, John. "Creativity Through Hatred—and a Few Thoughts on the Western Novel." *Western Review*, VI (Winter 1969), 12-7.

Bashford, Herbert. "The Literary Development of the Pacific Coast." *Atlantic Monthly*, XCII (1903), 1-9.

Boatright, Mody C. "The American Myth Rides the Range." *Southwest Review*, XXXVI (Summer 1951), 157-63.

Boatright, Mody C. "The American Rodeo." *American Quarterly*, XVI (Summer 1964), 195-202.

Boatright, Mody C. "The Beginnings of Cowboy Fiction." *Southwest Review*, LI (Winter 1966), 11-28.

Boatright, Mody C. "The Cowboy Enters the Movies." *The Sunny Slopes of Long Ago*. Texas Folklore Publications, XXXIII. Dallas, 1966, 51-69.

Boatright, Mody C. "The Formula in Cowboy Fiction and Drama." *Western Folklore*, XXVIII (April 1969), 136-45.

Boatright, Mody C. "The Myth of Frontier Individualism." *Southwestern Social Science Quarterly*, XXII (June 1941), 14-32.

Boatright, Mody C. "Literature in the Southwest." *Sul Ross State College Bulletin*, XXXIII (June 1, 1953), 1-32.

Bracher, Frederick. "California's Literary Regionalism." *American Quarterly*, VII (Fall 1955), 275-84.

Brashear, Minnie M. "Missouri Literature Since the First World War: Part III—The Novel." *Missouri Historical Review*, XLI (April 1947), 241-65.

Bredeson, Robert C. "Landscape Description in Nineteenth-Century American Travel Literature." *American Quarterly*, XX (1968), 86-94.

Byington, Robert. "The Frontier Hero: Refinement and Definition." *Publications of the Texas Folklore Society*, XXX (1960), 140-55.

Carroll, John Alexander. "Broader Approaches to the History of the West." *Arizona and the West*, I (Autumn 1959), 217-31.

Carstensen, Vernon. "Remarks on the Literary Treatment of the American Westward Movement." *Moderna Sprak*, LI (1957), 275-87.

Caughey, John W. "The American West: Frontier and Region." *Arizona and the West*, I (Spring 1959), 7-12.

Caughey, John W. "Shaping a Literary Tradition." *Pacific Historical Review*, XVIII (June 1939), 201-14. California literature.

Caughey, John W. "Toward an Understanding of the West." *Utah Historical Quarterly*, XXVII (January 1959), 7-24.

Cawelti, John. "Cowboys, Indians, Outlaws." *The American West*, I (Spring 1964), 28-35, 77-9.

Cawelti, John. "Prolegomena to the Western." *Studies in Public Communication*, IV (Autumn 1962), 57-70.

Cawelti, John G. "Prolegomena to the Western." *Western American Literature*, IV (Winter 1970), 259-71.

Clark, Thomas D. "The American Backwoodsman in Popular Portraiture." *Indiana Magazine of History*, XLII (1946), 1-28.

Clough, Wilson O. "The Cult of the Bad Man of the West." *Texas Quarterly*, V (Autumn 1962), 11-20.

Commager, Henry Steele. "The Literature of the Pioneer West." *Minnesota History*, VIII (December 1927), 319-28.

Cracroft, Richard E. "The American West of Karl May." *American Quarterly*, XIX (Summer 1967), 249-58.

Crowell, Chester T. "Cowboys." *American Mercury*, IX (October 1926), 162-9.

Current-Garcia, E. "Writers in the 'Sticks.' " *Prairie Schooner*, XII (Winter 1938), 294-309.

Dale, Edward E. "Culture on the American Frontier." *Nebraska History*, XXVI (1945), 75-90.

Dale, Edward E. "The Frontier Literary Society." *Nebraska History*, XXXI (1950), 167-82.

Dale, Edward Everett. "The Romance of the Range." *West Texas Historical Association Year Book*, V (June 1929), 3-22.

Davidson, Levette J. "Early Fiction of the Rocky Mountain Region." *Colorado Magazine*, X (1933), 161-72.

Davidson, Levette J. "Fact or Formula in 'Western' Fiction." *Colorado Quarterly*, III (Winter 1955), 278-87.

Davidson, Levette J. "Folk Elements in Midwestern Literature." *Western Humanities Review*, III (July 1949), 187-95.

Davidson, Levette J. "The Literature of Western America." *Western Humanities Review*, V (Spring 1951), 165-73.

Davis, David B. "Ten Gallon Hero." *American Quarterly*, VI (Summer 1954), 111-25.

Davis, Ronald L. "Culture on the Frontier." *Southwest Review*, LIII (1968), 383-403. Western drama.

Dessain, Kenneth. "Once in the Saddle: The Memory and Romance of the Trail Driving Cowboy." *Journal of Popular Culture*, IV (Fall 1970), 464-96.

Dippie, Brain W. "Bards of the Little Big Horn." *Western American Literature*, I (Fall 1966), 175-95.

Dobie, J. Frank. "Cow Country Tempo." *Texas Quarterly*, VII (Spring 1964), 30-6.

Donald, David and Frederick A. Palmer. "Toward a Western Literature, 1820-1860." *Mississippi Valley Historical Review*, XXXV (December 1948), 413-28.

Dondore, Dorothy. "Points of Contact Between History and Literature in the Mississippi Valley." *Mississippi Valley Historical Review*, XI (September 1924), 227-36.

15

Durham, Philip. "The Lost Cowboy." *Midwest Journal*, VII (1955), 176-82.

Durham, Philip. "The Negro Cowboy." *American Quarterly*, VII (1955), 291-301.

Durham, Philip. "Riders of the Plains: American Westerns." *Neuphilologische Mitteilungen*, LVIII (1957), 22-38.

Dykes, J. C. "Dime Novel Texas; or, the Sub-Literature of the Lone Star State." *The Southwestern Historical Quarterly*, XLIX (January 1946), 327-40.

Erno, Richard B. "The New Realism in Southwestern Literature." *Western Review*, VII (Spring 1970), 50-4.

Eshleman, H. D. "A Grownup Western at Last." *Colorado Quarterly*, XIX (Summer 1970), 107-12.

Etulain, Richard Wayne. "Recent Views of the American Literary West." *Journal of Popular Culture*, III (Summer 1969), 144-53.

Etulain, Richard W. "Recent Western Fiction." *Journal of the West*, VIII (October 1969), 656-8.

Fadiman, Clifton. "Party of One—The Literature of the Rockies." *Holiday*, XXXIV (August 1963), 10, 12-7.

Fife, Austin and Alta. "Spurs and Saddlebags: Ballads of the Cowboy." *The American West*, VII (September 1970), 44-7.

Fisher, Vardis. "The Western Writer and the Eastern Establishment." *Western American Literature*, I (Winter 1967), 244-59.

Fishwick, Marshall W. "The Cowboy: America's Contribution to the World's Mythology." *Western Folklore*, XI (April 1952), 77-92.

Flanagan, John T. "A Half-Century of Middlewestern Fiction." *Critique*, II (Winter 1959), 16-34.

Flanagan, John T. "Literary Protests in the Midwest." *Southwest Review*, XXXIV (Spring 1948), 148-57.

Flanagan, John T. "The Middle Western Farm Novel." *Minnesota History*, XXIII (June 1942), 113-47.

Flanagan, John T. "Thirty Years of Minnesota Fiction." *Minnesota History*, XXXI (September 1950), 129-47.

Folsom, James K. "English Westerns." *Western American Literature*, II (Spring 1967), 3-13.

Folsom, James K. "Shane and Hud: Two Stories in Search of a Medium." *Western Humanities Review*, XXIV (Autumn 1970), 359-72.

Folsom, James K. " 'Western' Themes and Western Films." *Western American Literature*, II (Fall 1967), 195-203.

Frederick, John T. "Early Iowa in Fiction." *Palimpsest*, XXXVI (October 1955), 389-420.

Frederick, John T. "The Farm in Iowa Fiction." *Palimpsest*, XXXII (March 1951), 124-52.

Frederick, John T. "Town and City in Iowa Fiction." *The Palimpsest*, XXXV (February 1954), 49-96.

French, Warren. "The Cowboy in the Dime Novel." *Texas Studies in English*, XXX (1951), 219-34.

French, Warren. "West as Myth: Status Report and Call for Action." *Western American Literature*, I (Spring 1966), 55-8.

Furness, Edna L. "Image of the Schoolteacher in Western Literature." *Arizona Quarterly*, XVIII (Winter 1962), 346-57.

Garland, Hamlin. "Literary Emancipation of the West." *Forum*, XVI (1893), 156-66.

Garland, Hamlin. "The West in Literature." *Arena*, VI (1892), 669-76.

Gaston, Edwin W., Jr. "Travel Accounts of the Southern Plains: 1800-1850." *The Texas Journal of Science*, XI (March 1959), 3-16.

Gohdes, Clarence. "The Earliest Description of 'Western' Fiction?" *American Literature*, XXXVII (March 1965), 70-1.

Gillmor, Frances. "Southwestern Chronicle from Report to Literature." *Arizona Quarterly*, XII (Winter 1956), 344-51.

Goodwyn, Frank. "The Frontier in American Fiction." *Revista Interamericana de Bibliografía: Inter-American Review of Bibliography*, X (1960), 356-69.

Greene, Donald. "Western Canadian Literature." *Western American Literature*, II (Winter 1968), 257-280.

Gurian, Jay. "The Possibility of a Western Poetics." *Colorado Quarterly*, XV (Summer 1966), 69-85.

Gurian, Jay. "Sweetwater Journalism and Western Myth." *Annals of Wyoming*, XXXVI (1964), 79-88.

Gurian, Jay. "The Unwritten West." *The American West*, II (Winter 1965), 59-63.

Guthrie, Alfred B., Jr. "The Historical Novel." *Montana Magazine of History*, IV (Fall 1954), 1-8.

Hale, Edward E. "The Romantic Landscape of the Far West." *Union College Bulletin*, XXIII (January 1930), 5-17.

Haslam, Gerald. "American Indians: Poets of the Cosmos." *Western American Literature*, V (Spring 1970), 15-29.

Haslam, Gerald. "American Literature: Some Forgotten Pages." *ETC: A Review of General Semantics*, XVII (June 1970), 221-38.

Haslam, Gerald. "Por La Causa! Mexican-American Literature." *College English*, XXXI (April 1970), 695-709.

Heilman, Robert B. "The Western Theme: Exploiters and Explorers." *Northwest Review*, IV (Fall-Winter 1960), 5-14.

Hertzel, Leo J. "What About Writers in the North?" *South Dakota Review*, V (Spring 1967), 3-19.

Hitt, Helen. "History in Pacific Northwest Novels Written Since 1920." *Oregon Historical Quarterly*, LI (September 1950), 180-206.

Holbrook, Stewart H. *Far Corner: A Personal View of the Pacific Northwest*. New York: The Macmillan Company, 1952, 220-30.

Horgan, Paul. "The Cowboy Revisited." *Southwest Review*, XXXIX (Autumn 1954), 285-97.

Hornberger, Theodore. "Three Self-Conscious Wests." *Southwest Review*, XXVI (July 1941), 428-48.

Hough, Emerson. "The West, and Certain Literary Discoveries." *Century*, LIX (February 1900), 506-11.

Howard, Leon. "Literature and the Frontier." *English Literary History*, VII (1940), 68-82.

Hubbell, Jay B. "The Frontier in American Literature." *Southwest Review*, X (January 1925), 84-92.

Hunsaker, Kenneth B. "Mid-Century Mormon Novels." *Dialogue: A Journal of Mormon Thought*, IV (Autumn 1969), 123-8.

Hutchinson, W. H. "Virgins, Villains, and Varmints." *Huntington Library Quarterly*, XVI (August 1953), 381-92.

Hutchinson, W. H. "The Western Story as Literature." *Western Humanities Review*, III (January 1949), 33-7.

James, Stuart B. "Western American Space and the Human Imagination." *Western Humanities Review*, XXIV (Spring 1970), 147-55.

Jewett, Isaac Appleton. "Themes for Western Fiction." *The Western Monthly Magazine*, I (December 1833), 574-88.

Jones, Harry H. "The Mining Theme in Western Fiction." *Studies in the Literature of the West*. Laramie: University of Wyoming, 1956, 101-29.

Jones, Margaret Ann. "The Cowboy and Ranching in Magazine Fiction, 1901-1910" *Studies in the Literature of the West*. Laramie: University of Wyoming, 1956, 57-74.

Josephy, Alvin M., Jr. "Publishers' Interests in Western Writing." *Western American Literature*, I (Winter 1967), 260-6.

Juricek, J. T. "American Usage of the Word 'Frontier' from Colonial Times to Frederick Jackson Turner." *Proceedings of the American Philosophical Society*, CX (February 18, 1966), 10-34.

Keeler, Clinton. "Children of Innocence: The Agrarian Crusade in Fiction." *Western Humanities Review*, VI (Autumn 1952), 363-76.

Keim, Charles J. "Writing the Great Alaska Novel." *Alaska Review*, III (Fall-Winter 1969), 47-51.

Keleher, Julia. "Los Paisanos." *New Mexico Quarterly Review*, XV (Summer 1945), 260-3.

Keller, Karl. "On Words and the Word of God: The Delusions of a Mormon Literature." *Dialogue: A Journal of Mormon Thought,* IV (Autumn 1969), 13-20.

King, James T. "The Sword and the Pen: The Poetry of the Military Frontier." *Nebraska History,* XLVII (September 1966), 229-45.

Kizer, Carolyn. "Poetry: School of the Pacific Northwest." *New Republic,* CXXXV (July 16, 1956), 18-9.

Krause, Herbert. "Myth and Reality on the High Plains." *South Dakota Review,* I (December 1963), 3-20.

Lambert, Neal E. "Freedom and the American Cowboy." *Brigham Young University Studies,* VIII (1967 / 68), 61-71.

Lambert, Neal. "Saints, Sinners and Scribes: A Look at the Mormons in Fiction." *Utah Historical Quarterly,* XXXVI (Winter 1968), 63-76.

Lavender, David. "The Petrified West and the Writer." *The American Scholar,* XXXVII (Spring 1968), 293-306.

Leach, Joseph. "The Paper-Back Texan: Father of the American Western Hero." *Western Humanities Review,* XI (1957), 267-75.

Leithead, J. Edward. "The Saga of Young Wild West." *American Book Collector,* XIX (March 1969), 17-22.

Lewis, Marvin. "A Free Life in the Mines and on the Range." *Western Humanities Review,* XII (Winter 1958), 87-95.

Lyon, Peter. "The Wild, Wild West." *American Heritage,* XI (August 1960), 32-48.

McDowell, Tremaine. "Regionalism in the United States." *Minnesota History,* XX (June 1939), 105-18.

McWilliams, Cary. "Myths of the West." *North American Review,* CCXXXII (November 1931), 424-32.

McWilliams, Carey. "The West: A Lost Chapter." *Frontier,* XII (November 1932), 15-24.

Marchand, Ernest. "Emerson and the Frontier." *American Literature,* III (May 1931), 149-74.

Marks, Barry. "The Concept of Myth in *Virgin Land.*" *American Quarterly,* V(Spring 1953), 71-6.

Meyer, Roy W. "Character Types in Literature About the American West." *Opinion,* XIII (December 1969), 21-9.

Meyer, Roy W. "The Outback and the West: Australian and American Frontier Fiction." *Western American Literature,* VI (Spring 1971), 3-19.

Meyer, Roy W. "The Scandinavian Immigrant in American Farm Fiction." *American Scandinavian Review,* XLVII (September 1959), 243-9.

Meyer, Roy W. "Naturalism in American Farm Fiction." *Journal of the Central Mississippi Valley American Studies Association,* II (Spring 1961), 27-37.

Miles, Josephine. "Pacific Coast Poetry, 1947." *Pacific Spectator,* II (1948), 134-50.

Millbrook, Minnie D. "The West Breaks in General Custer." *The Kansas Historical Quarterly,* XXXVI (Summer 1970), 113-48.

Milton, John R. "The American Novel: The Search for Home, Tradition and Identity." *Western Humanities Review,* XVI (Spring 1962), 169-80.

Milton, John R. "The American West: A Challenge to the Literary Imagination." *Western American Literature,* I (Winter 1967), 267-84.

Milton, John. "Earth and Sky: Fiction for Our Time." *Bulletin of Jamestown College,* XLIX (December 31, 1958), 1-4.

Milton, John. "Fact and Fantasy in Western Fiction." *South Dakota Library Bulletin,* XLVIII (December 1962), 126-30.

Milton, John R. "Inside the *South Dakota Review.*" *Midcontinent American Studies Journal,* X (Fall 1969), 68-78.

Milton, John R. "The Novel in the American West." *South Dakota Review,* II (Autumn 1964), 56-76.

Milton, John R., ed. "The Western Novel—A Symposium." *South Dakota Review,* II (Autumn 1964), 3-36.

Milton, John R. "The Western Novel: Sources and Forms." *Chicago Review,* XVI (Summer 1963), 74-100.

Monaghan, Jay. "The West in Fiction." *American Library Association Bulletin,* XLVIII (1954), 94-9.

Morgan, Dale L. "Literature in the History of the Church: The Importance of Involvement." *Dialogue: A Journal of Mormon Thought,* IV (Autumn 1969), 26-32.

Morley, S. Griswold. "Cowboy and Gaucho Fiction." *New Mexico Quarterly,* XVI (Autumn 1946), 253-67.

Norell, Irene P. "Prose Writers of North Dakota." *North Dakota Quarterly,* XXVI (Winter 1958), 1-36.

Oliver, Egbert S. "The Pig-tailed China Boys Out West." *Western Humanities Review,* XII (1958), 159-78.

Paine, Gregory. "The Frontier in American Literature." *Sewanee Review,* XXXVI (1928), 225-36.

Pearce, T. M. "The Un-Static Southwest." *Southwestern American Literature,* I (January 1971), 1-3.

Pearce, T. M. "The 'Other' Frontiers of the American West." *Arizona and the West,* IV (Summer 1962), 105-12.

Peterson, Levi S. "The Primitive and the Civilized in Western Fiction." *Western American Literature,* I (Fall 1966), 197-207.

Peyroutet, Jean A. "The North Dakota Farmer in Fiction." *North Dakota Quarterly,* XXXIX (Winter 1971), 59-71.

Phillips, James E. "Arcadia on the Range." *Themes and Directions in American Literature: Essays in Honor of Leon Howard*, eds. Ray B. Browne and Donald Pizer. Lafayette: Purdue University Studies, 1969, pp. 108-29.

Pilkington, W. T. "The Recent Southwestern Novel." *Southwestern American Literature*, I (January 1971), 12-5.

Pilkington, William T. "Aspects of the Western Comic Novel." *Western American Literature*, I (Fall 1966), 209-17.

Pollard, Lancaster. "Washington Literature: A Historical Sketch." *Pacific Northwest Quarterly*, XXIX (1938), 227-54.

Polos, Nicholas C. "Early California Poetry." *California Historical Society Quarterly*, XLVIII (September 1969), 243-55.

Pomeroy, Earl. "Old Lamps for New: The Cultural Lag in Pacific Coast Historiography." *Arizona and the West*, II (Summer 1960), 107-26.

Pomeroy, Earl. "Rediscovering the West." *American Quarterly*, XII (Spring 1960), 20-30.

Pomeroy, Earl. "Towards a Reorientation of Western History." *Mississippi Valley Historical Review*, XLI (March 1955), 579-600.

Povey, John F. "A New Second-Language Indian Literature." *Alaska Review*, III (Fall-Winter 1969), 73-8.

Redekip, Ernest. "The Redmen: Some Representatives of Indians in American Literature Before the Civil War." *Canadian Association for American Studies Bulletin*, III (Winter 1968), 1-44.

Rudolph, Earle Leighton. "The Frontier in American Literature." *Jahrbuch für Amerikastudien*, VII (1962), 77-91.

Rundell, Walter, Jr. "Concepts of the 'Frontier' and the 'West.' " *Arizona and the West*, I (Spring 1959), 13-41.

Schein, Harry. "The Olympian Cowboy." *American Scholar*, XXIV (Summer 1955), 309-20.

Schwartz, Joseph. "The Wild West Show: 'Everything Genuine.' " *Journal of Popular Culture*, III (Spring 1970), 656-66.

Scullin, George. "The Old Wild West." *Cosmopolitan*, CXLV (November 1958), 48-55.

Shaul, Lawana J. "The West in Magazine Fiction, 1870-1900." *Studies in the Literature of the West*. Laramie: University of Wyoming, 1956, 29-56.

Sherman, Caroline B. "The Development of American Rural Fiction." *Agricultural History*, XII (January 1938), 67-76.

Sherman, Caroline B. "Farm Life Fiction." *South Atlantic Quarterly*, XXVII (July 1928), 310-24.

Sherman, Caroline B. "Rural Literature Faces Peace." *South Atlantic Quarterly*, XLII (January 1943), 59-71.

Smith, Duane Allan. "Mining Camps: Myth vs. Reality." *Colorado Magazine*, XLIV (Spring 1967), 93-110.

Smith, Edwin B. " 'The Confused West': A Literary Forecast." *Essays and Addresses*, Chicago, 1909, 360-76.

Smith, Goldie Capers. "*The Overland Monthly*: Landmark in American Literature." *New Mexico Quarterly*, XXXIII (Autumn 1963), 333-40.

Smith, Henry Nash. "Can 'American Studies' Develop a Method?" *American Quarterly*, IX (Summer 1957), 197-208.

Smith, Henry Nash. "The Dime Novel Heroine." *Southwest Review*, XXXIV (Spring 1949), 182-8.

Smith, Henry N. "The Frontier Hypothesis and the Myth of the West." *American Quarterly*, II (1950), 3-11.

Smith, Henry Nash. "Kit Carson in Books." *Southwest Review*, XXVIII (Winter 1943), 164-90.

Smith, Henry Nash. "Origins of Native American Literary Tradition." *The American Writer and the European*, eds. Margaret Denny and William H. Gibson. Minneapolis: University of Minnesota Press, 1950, 63-77.

Smith, Henry Nash. "The West as an Image of the American Past." *The University of Kansas City Review*, XVIII (Autumn 1951), 29-40.

Smith, Henry Nash. "Western Chroniclers and Literary Pioneers." in Robert E. Spiller, *et al. Literary History of the United States*. 3 vols. New York: Macmillan, 1948.

Smith, Henry Nash. "The Western Farmer in Imaginative Literature, 1818-1891." *Mississippi Valley Historical Review*, XXXVI (December 1949), 479-90.

Smith, Henry Nash. "The Western Hero in the Dime Novel." *Southwest Review*, XXXIII (Summer 1948), 276-84.

Smith, Rebecca W. "The Southwest in Fiction." *Saturday Review*, XXV (May 16, 1942), 12-3, 37.

Sonnichsen, C. L. "Fiction and History." *Mountain-Plains Library Quarterly*, XIII (Summer 1968), 3-9.

Sonnichsen, C. L. "The New Style Western." *South Dakota Review*, IV (Summer 1966), 22-8.

Sonnichsen, C. L. "The Wyatt Earp Syndrome." *The American West*, VII (May 1970), 26-8, 60-2.

Steckmesser, Kent L. "Custer in Fiction." *The American West*, I (Fall 1964), 47-52, 63-4.

Steckmesser, . Kent L. "Paris and the Wild West." *Southwest Review*, LIV (Spring 1969), 168-74.

Steensma, Robert C. " 'Stay Right There and Toughy It Out': The American Homesteader as Autobiographer." *Western Review*, VI (Spring 1969), 10-8.

Stegner, Wallace. "Born a Square—The Westernerners' Dilemna." *Atlantic*, CCXIII (January 1964), 46-50.

Stegner, Wallace. "Commentary: A Matter of Continuity." *American West Review*, I (December 1967), 12.

Stegner, Wallace. "History, Myth and the Western Writer." *The American West*, IV (May 1967), 61-2, 76-9.

Stevenson, Dorothy. "The Battle for Buckshot Basin." *New Mexico Quarterly*, XXXIII (Autumn 1963), 315-24.

Stewart, George R. "The West as Seen from the East (1800-1850)." *Pacific Spectator*, I (1947), 188-95.

Straight, Michael. "Truth and Formula for the Western Novel." *South Dakota Review*, II (Autumn 1964), 88-93.

Swallow, Alan. "A Magazine for the West?" *Inland*, I (Autumn 1957), 3-6.

Swallow, Alan. "The Mavericks." *Critique*, II (Winter 1959), 74-92.

Swallow, Alan. "Poetry of the West." *South Dakota Review*, II (Autumn 1964), 77-87.

Taylor, J. Golden. "The Western Short Story." *South Dakota Review*, II (Autumn 1964), 37-55.

Tenfelde, Nancy L. "New Frontiers Revisited." *Midwest Review*, IV (1962), 54-62.

Todd, Edgeley W. "James Hall and the Hugh Glass Legend." *American Quarterly*, VII (Winter 1955), 363-70.

Todd, Edgeley W. "A Note on 'The Mountain Man as Literary Hero.'" *Western American Literature*, I (Fall 1966), 219-21.

Torres-Rioseco, Arturo. "The Twenty-Five Year Anniversary of Don Segundo Sombra." *New Mexico Quarterly*, XXI (Autumn 1951), 274-80. Deals with the South American cowboy novel.

Van Doren, Mark. "Repudiation of the Pioneer." *English Journal*, XVIII (October 1928), 616-23.

Veysey, Laurence R. "Myth and Reality in Approaching American Regionalism." *American Quarterly*, XII (Spring 1960), 31-43. In part a critique of H. N. Smith's *Virgin Land*.

Waldmeir, J.J. "The Cowboy, Knight and Popular Taste." *Southern Folklore Quarterly*, XXII (September 1958), 113-20.

Walker, Don D. "Freedom and Destiny in the Myth of the American West." *New Mexico Quarterly*, XXXIII (Winter 1963-64), 381-7.

Walker, Don D. "The Mountain Man as Literary Hero." *Western American Literature*, I (Spring 1966), 15-25.

Walker, Don D. "Reading on the Range: The Literary Habits of the American Cowboy." *Arizona and the West*, II (Winter 1960), 307-18.

Walker, Don D. "The Rise and Fall of Barney Tullus." *Western American Literature*, III (Summer 1968), 93-102. All students of western literature should read this essay.

Walker, Robert H. "The Poets Interpret the Western Frontier." *Mississippi Valley Historical Review*, XLVII (1961), 619-35.

Warren, Sidney. *Farthest Frontier: The Pacific Northwest.* New York: The Macmillan Company, 1949, 242-74.

Warshaw, Robert. "The Westerner." *Partisan Review*, XXI (March 1954), 190-203.

Weaver, John D. "The Antic Arts—The Western Hero." *Holiday*, XXXIV (August 1963), 77-80 ff.

Webb, Walter P. "The American West: Perpetual Mirage." *Harper's*, CCXIV (May 1957), 25-31.

Webb, Walter P. "The Great Frontier and Modern Literature." *Southwest Review*, XXXVII (Spring 1952), 85-100.

West, Ray B., Jr. "Four Rocky Mountain Novels." *Rocky Mountain Review*, X (Autumn 1945), 21-8.

Westbrook, Max. "Conservative, Liberal, and Western: Three Modes of American Realism." *South Dakota Review*, IV (Summer 1966), 3-19.

Westbrook, Max. "The Practical Spirit: Sacrality and the American West." *Western American Literature*, III (Fall 1968), 193-205.

Westbrook, Max. "The Themes of Western Fiction." *Southwest Review*, XLIII (Summer 1958), 232-8.

Westermeier, Clifford P. "The Cowboy—Sinner or Saint." *New Mexico Historical Review*, XXV (April 1950), 89-108.

White, Helen C. "The Writing of Historical Romance." *Wisconsin Magazine of History*, XL (Winter 1956-57), 83-6.

Wiebe, Rudy. "Western Canada Fiction: Past and Future." *Western American Literature*, VI (Spring 1971), 21-30.

Williams, John. "The 'Western': Definition of the Myth." *Nation*, CXCIII (November 18, 1961), 401-6.

Willson, Lawrence. "The Transcendentalist View of the West." *Western Humanities Review*, XIV (1960), 183-91.

"Writing in the West and Midwest." *Critique*, II (Winter 1959), 1-97.

Young, Vernon. "An American Dream and Its Parody." *Arizona Quarterly*, VI (Summer 1950), 112-23.

Zanger, Jules. "The Frontiersman in Popular Fiction." in J. F. McDermott, ed. *The Frontier Re-Examined.* Urbana: University of Illinois Press, 1968.

THREE TOPICS

I. THE BEATS

Bingham, June. "The Intelligent Square's Guide to Hippieland." *The New York Times Magazine*, VI (September 24, 1967), 25, 68-73, 76-84.

Charters, Ann, ed. *Scenes Along the Road: Photographs of the Desolation Angels, 1944-1960.* Gotham Book Mart, 1970.

Ciardi, John. "Epitaph for the Dead Beats." *Saturday Review*, XLIII (February 6, 1960), 11-13.

Cook, Bruce. *The Beat Generation.* New York: Charles Scribners, 1971.

Feldman, Gene and Max Gartenberg, eds. *The Beat Generation and the Angry Young Men.* New York: Citadel Press, 1958.

Ferlinghetti, Lawrence, ed. *Beatitude Anthology.* San Francisco: City Lights Books, 1960.

Holmes, John C. *Nothing More to Declare.* New York: E. P. Dutton, 1967.

Kheridian, David. *Six Poets of the San Francisco Renaissance.* Fresno: The Giligia Press, 1967.

Krim, Seymour, ed. *The Beats.* New York: Fawcett Publications, 1960.

Lipton, Lawrence. "Disaffiliation and the Art of Poverty." *Chicago Review*, X (Spring 1956), 53-79.

Lipton, Lawrence. *The Holy Barbarians.* New York, 1959.

Parkinson, Thomas, ed. *A Casebook on the Beat.* New York: Thomas Y. Crowell Company, 1961.

Parkinson, Thomas. "After the Beat Generation." *Colorado Quarterly*, XVII (1968), 45-56.

Parkinson, Thomas. "Phenomenon or Generation." *A Casebook on the Beat.* New York: Thomas Y. Crowell, 1961.

Podhoretz, Norman. "The Know-Nothing Bohemians." *Partisan Review*, XXV (Spring 1958), 305-11, 313-6, 318.

Rexroth, Kenneth. *The Alternative Society: Essays from the Other World.* New York: Herder and Herder, 1970.

Rexroth, Kenneth. "Disengagement: The Art of the Beat Generation." *New World Writing No. 11.* New York: The New American Library, 1957.

Rexroth, Kenneth. "San Francisco's Mature Bohemians." *Nation*, CLXXXIV (February 23, 1957), 157-62.

Sisk, John P. "Beatnicks and Tradition." *Commonweal*, LXX (April 17, 1959), 74-7.

Wilentz, Ellias, ed. *The Beat Scene.* New York: Citadel Press / Corinth Books, 1960.

II. LOCAL COLOR AND REGIONALISM

Allen, Charles. "Regionalism and the Little Magazines." *College English*, VII (1945), 10-6.

Austin, Mary. "Regionalism in American Fiction." *English Journal*, XXI (1932), 97-107.

Baker, Joseph E. "Four Arguments for Regionalism." *Saturday Review*, XV (November 28, 1936), 3-4, 14.

Baker, Joseph E. "Provinciality." *College English*, I (1940), 488-94.

Baker, Joseph E. "Regionalism in the Middle West." *The American Review*, IV (March 1935), 603-14.

Baker, Joseph E. "Western Man Against Nature." *College English*, IV (October 1942), 19-26.

Benton, Thomas H. "American Regionalism: A Personal History of the Movement." *University of Kansas City Review*, XVII (Autumn 1951), 41-75.

Bernard, Harry. *Le Roman régionaliste aux Étas-Unis, 1913-1940.* Montreal: Editions Fides, 1949.

Botkin, Benjamin A. "Regionalism: Cult or Culture?" *English Journal*, XXV (March 1936), 181-5.

Botkin, Benjamin A. "We Talk about Regionalism—North, East, South and West." *Frontier*, XIII (May 1933), 286-96.

Bracher, Frederick. "California's Literary Regionalism." *American Quarterly*, VII (Fall 1955), 275-84.

Brasher, Minnie M. "Missouri Literature Since the First World War: Part III—The Novel." *Missouri Historical Review*, XLI (April 1947), 241-65.

Brodin, Pierre. *Le Roman Régionaliste Americain.* Paris, 1937.

Brooks, Cleanth. "Regionalism in American Literature." *Journal of Southern History*, XXVI (Fall 1960), 35-43.

Coleman, Rufus A. "Literature and the Region." *Pacific Northwest Quarterly*, XXXIX (1948), 312-8.

Davidson, Donald. "Regionalism and Nationalism in American Literature." *American Review*, V (1935), 48-61.

Dike, Donald A. "Notes on Local Color and Its Relation to Realism." *College English*, XIV (November 1952), 81-8.

Dobie, J. Frank. "The Writer and His Region." *Southwest Review*, XXXV (1950), 81-7.

Dondore, Dorothy. "Points of Contact Between History and Literature in the Mississippi Valley." *Mississippi Valley Historical Review*, XI (September 1924), 227-36.

DuBois, Arthur E. "Among the Quarterlies: The Question of 'Regionalism.' " *Sewanee Review*, XLV (1937), 216-27.

Eichelberger, Clayton. "Relation of Local Color to the Range Fiction of Wister, Lewis, and Rhodes." Unpublished master's thesis, University of Colorado, 1950.

Fisher, Vardis. "The Novelist and His Background." *Western Folklore*, XII (1953), 1-8.

Fishwick, Marshall. "What Ever Happened to Regionalism?" *Southern Humanities Review*, II (Fall 1968), 393-401.

Fiske, Horace S. *Provincial Types in American Fiction*. New York, 1903.

Flanagan, John T. "The Middle Western Farm Novel." *Minnesota History*, XXIII (June 1942), 113-47.

Flanagan, John T. "Middlewestern Regional Literature." *Research Opportunities in American Cultural History*, ed. John Francis McDermott. Lexington: University of Kentucky Press, 1961, 124-39.

Flanagan, John T. "Some Middlewestern Literary Magazines." *Papers on Language and Literature*, III (Summer 1967), 237-53.

Gohdes, Clarence. "Exploitation of the Provinces." *The Literature of the American People*, ed. Arthur H. Quinn. New York, 1951, 639-60.

Hakac, John. "Southwestern Regional Material in a Literature Class." *Western Review*, VII (Spring 1970), 12-8.

Harkness, David James. *The Literary Midwest*. University of Tennessee News Letter, XXXVII (February 1958).

Hubbell, Jay B. "The Decay of the Provinces." *Sewanee Review*, XXXV (1927), 473-87.

Jensen, Merrill, ed. *Regionalism in America*. Madison: University of Wisconsin Press, 1951; 1965.

Johnson, Thomas. "Regionalism and Local Color." *Literary History of the U.S.* New York, 1948, Vol. 3, 304-25; 3d ed., 1963, Vol. 2, 304-25.

Keller, Richard Morton. "Regionalism in the Novels of the Northwest." Unpublished master's thesis, State College of Washington, 1938.

Kellock, Katharine. "The WPA Writers: Portraitists of the United States." *American Scholar*, IX (1940), 473-82.

Mabie, Hamilton W. "Provincialism in American Life." *Harper's*, CXXXIV (1917), 579-84; *American Ideals, Character and Life*. New York, 1913, 91-127.

McCleod, Norman, *et al.* "Regionalism: A Symposium." *Sewanee Review*, XXXIX (October-December 1931), 456-83.

McDowell, Tremaine. "Regionalism in American Literature." *Minnesota History*, XX (June 1939), 105-18.

McWilliams, Carey. "Localism in American Criticism, a Century and a Half of Controversy." *Southwest Review*, XIX (1934), 410-28.

McWilliams, Carey. *The New Regionalism in American Literature.* Seattle, 1930.

Odum, Howard W., and Harry Estill Moore. *American Regionalism.* New York: Henry Holt and Co., 1938.

Oldham, John N. "Anatomy of Provincialism." *Sewanee Review,* XLIV (1936), 68-75, 144-52, 296-302.

Radke, Merle L. "Local-Color Fiction in Middle-Western Magazines, 1865-1900." Unpublished doctoral dissertation, Northwestern University, 1965.

Ransom, John C. "The Aesthetic of Regionalism." *American Review,* II (1934), 290-310.

Rhode, Robert D. "The Functions of Setting in the American Short Story of Local Color, 1865-1900." Unpublished doctoral dissertation, University of Texas, 1940.

Rhode, Robert D. "Scenery and Setting: A Note on American Local Color." *College English,* XIII (December 1951), 142-6.

Rovit, Earl H. "The Regions versus the Nation: Critical Battle of the Thirties." *Mississippi Quarterly,* XIII (Spring 1960), 90-8.

Saum, L. O. "The Success Theme in Great Plains Realism." *American Quarterly,* XVIII (1966), 579-98.

Simpson, Claude M., ed. *The Local Colorists: American Short Stories, 1857-1900.* New York: Harper and Brothers, 1960.

Skelley, Grant Teasdale. "The *Overland Monthly* under Millicent Washburn Shinn, 1883-1894: A Study of Regional Publishing." Unpublished doctoral dissertation, University of California, Berkeley, 1968.

Spencer, Benjamin T. "Nationality During the Interregnum." *American Literature,* XXXII (January 1961), 434-45.

Spencer, Benjamin T. *The Quest for Nationality: An American Literary Campaign.* Syracuse, 1957.

Spencer, Benjamin T. "Regionalism in American Literature." *Regionalism in America.* Madison: University of Wisconsin Press, 1952, 219-60.

Stearns, Bertha-Monica. "Literary Rivalry and Local Books (1836-1860)." *Americana,* XXX (January 1936), 7-19.

Stewart, George R. "The Regional Approach to Literature." *College English,* IX (April 1948), 370-5.

Suckow, Ruth. "Middle Western Literature." *English Journal,* XXI (March 1932), 175-81.

Tate, Allen. "The New Provincialism . . ." *Virginia Quarterly Review,* XXI (1945), 262-72.

Towards a Native Rural Culture: American Regional Literature . . . Madison, Wisconsin, 1941.

Tuppet, Mary M. "A History of *The Southwest Review:* Toward an Understanding of Regionalism." Unpublished doctoral dissertation, University of Illinois, 1966.

Veysey, Lawrence. "Myth and Reality in Approaching Western Regionalism." *American Quarterly,* XII (Spring 1960), 31-43.

Walcutt, Charles C. "The Regional Novel and Its Future." *Arizona Quarterly,* I (Summer 1945), 17-27.

Walcutt, Charles C. "Regionalism—Practical or Aesthetic?" *Sewanee Review,* XLIX (1941), 165-72.

Walterhouse, Roger R. *Bret Harte, Joaquin Miller, and the Western Local Color Story.* Chicago: University of Chicago, 1939.

Warfel, Harry R., and G. Harrison Orians. *American Local-Color Stories.* New York: American Book Company, 1941.

Warren, Robert P. "Some Don'ts for Literary Regionalists." *American Review,* VIII (1936), 142-50.

Williams, Cecil B. "The American Local Color Movement and Its Cultural Significance." *Oklahoma State University Publications,* XLVIII (September 30, 1951), 5-13.

Williams, Cecil B. "Regionalism in American Literature." *Geist Einer Freien Gesellschaft,* Heidelberg: Verlag Quelle and Meyer, 1962, 331-87.

Winther, Sophus K. "The Limits of Regionalism." *Arizona Quarterly,* VIII (Spring 1952) 30-6.

III. THE WESTERN

Agnew, Seth M. "Destry Goes on Riding—or—Working the Six-Gun Lode." *Publisher's Weekly,* CLXII (1952), 746-51.

Agnew, Seth. "God's Country and the Publisher." *Saturday Review,* XXXVI (March 14, 1953), 26-7.

Agnew, Seth M. "The Literary Tumbleweed." *Saturday Review,* XXXVI (March 27, 1954), 15 ff.

Barker, Warren J., M.D. "The Stereotyped Western Story: Its Latent Meaning and Psychoeconomic Function." *Psychoanalytic Quarterly,* XXIV (June 1955), 270-80.

Barsness, John A. "The Breaking of a Myth: A Study of Cultural Implications in the Development of the Western Novel in the Twentieth Century." Unpublished doctoral dissertation, University of Minnesota, 1968.

Bennett, M. H. "The Scenic West: Silent Mirage." *Colorado Quarterly,* VIII (Summer 1959), 15-25.

Birney, Hoffman. "A Year-End Roundup on the Western Range." *NYTBR* (December 4, 1955), 38.

Bluestone, George. "The Changing Cowboy: From Dime Novel to Dollar Film" *Western Humanities Review,* XIV (Summer 1960), 331-7.

Boatright, Mody C. "The American Myth Rides the Range." *Southwest Review,* XXXVI (Summer 1951), 157-63.

Boatright, Mody C. "The Beginnings of Cowboy Fiction." *Southwest Review,* LI (Winter 1966), 11-28.

Boatright, Mody C. "The Formula in Cowboy Fiction and Drama." *Western Folklore,* XXVIII (April 1969), 136-45.

Branch, Edward Douglas. *The Cowboy and His Interpreters.* New York: D. Appleton and Co., 1926.

Brashers, Howard C. "The Cowboy Story from Stereotype to Art." *Moderna Sprak,* LVII (1963), 290-9.

Burack, A. S., ed. *The Craft of Novel Writing.* Boston: The Writer, Inc., 1948, pp. 179-89.

Capps, Benjamin. "The Promise of Western Fiction." *The Roundup,* XVII (October 1969), 1-2, 20; (November 1969), 2, 4, 14; (December 1969), 6, 8, 24.

Cawelti, John. "Cowboys, Indians, Outlaws: The West in Myth and Fantasy." *The American West,* I (Spring 1964), 28-35, 77-9.

Cawelti, John G. "The Gunfighter and Society." *The American West,* V (March 1968), 30-5, 76-8.

Cawelti, John. "Prolegomena to the Western." *Studies in Public Communication,* IV (Autumn 1962), 57-70.

Cawelti, John G. "Prolegomena to the Western." *Western American Literature,* VI (Winter 1970), 259-71.

Cawelti, John. "Recent Trends in the Study of Popular Culture." *American Studies: An International Newsletter,* X (Winter 1971), 23-37. Includes helpful bibliography.

Cawelti, John. *The Six-Gun Mystique.* Bowling Green, Ohio: Bowling Green University Popular Press, 1971.

Cronin, Con P. "Arizona's Six Gun Classic." *Arizona Historical Review,* III (July 1930), 7-11.

Cunningham Eugene. "Better Westerns." *Writer,* LIII (April 1940), 105-8.

Davidson, Levette J. "Fact or Formula in 'Western' Fiction." *Colorado Quarterly,* III (Winter 1955), 278-87.

Davis, David B. "Ten Gallon Hero." *American Quarterly,* VI (Summer 1954), 111-25.

Derleth, August W. "Romantic Story." *Writing Fiction.* Boston: The Writer, Inc., 1946.

DeVoto, Bernard. "Birth of an Art." *Harper's,* CCXI (December 1955), 8-9, 12, 14, 16.

DeVoto, Bernard. "Phaëthon on Gunsmoke Trail." *Harper's,* CCIX (December 1954), 10-11, 14, 16.

DeVoto, Bernard. "Horizon Land (1)." *Saturday Review*, XIV (October 17, 1936), 8; "Horizon Land (2)." *Saturday Review*, XV (April 24, 1937), 8.

Durham, Philip. "The Cowboy and the Myth Makers." *Journal of Popular Culture*, I (Summer 1967), 58-62.

Durham, Philip. "The Negro Cowboy." *American Quarterly*, VII (Fall 1955), 291-301.

Durham, Philip. "Riders of the Plains: American Westerns." *Neuphilologische Mitteilungen*, LVIII (November 1957), 22-38.

Durham, Philip, and Everett L. Jones. "The West as Fiction." *The Negro Cowboys*, New York: Dodd, Mead and Company, 1965, 220-30.

Dykes, J. C. "High Spots of Western Fiction: 1902-1952." *Westerners Brand Book*, XII (September 1955), 49-56.

Etulain, Richard W. "Literary Historians and the Western." *Journal of Popular Culture*, IV (Fall 1970), 518-26.

Etulain, Richard. "Three Western Novels." *Journal of the West*, X (April 1971), 389-90.

Eyles, Allen. *The Western*. New York: A. S. Barnes & Co., 1967.

Fenin, George N., and William K. Everson. *The Western: From Silents to Cinerama*. New York: Bonanza Books, 1962.

Fishwick, Marshall W. "The Cowboy: America's Contribution to the World's Mythology." *Western Folklore*, XI (April 1952), 77-92.

Fishwick, Marshall W. "Daniel Boone and the Pattern of the Western Hero." *Filson Club Historical Quarterly*, XXVII (1953), 119-38.

Folsom, James K. *The American Western Novel*. New Haven: College and University Press, 1966.

Franklin, Elisa. "Westerns, First and Lasting." *Quarterly of Film, Radio, and Television*, VII (Winter 1952), 109-15.

Frederick, John T. "Worthy Westerns." *English Journal*, XLIII (September 1954), 281-6, 296.

French, Warren. "West as Myth: Status Report and Call for Action." *Western American Literature*, I (Spring 1966), 55-8.

Gardner, Erle Stanley. "My Stories of the Wild West." *The Atlantic Monthly*, CCXVIII (July 1966), 60-2.

Garfield, Brian. "The Sun God Myth." *The Roundup*, XIII (July 1965), 9.

Garfield, Brian. "The Western Hero's Eden." *The Roundup*, XIII (September 1965), 1-2.

Garfield, Brian. "What Is the 'Formula'?" *The Roundup*, XIII (August 1968), 1-2.

Goldstein, Bernice, and Robert Perrucci. "The TV Western and the Modern American Spirit." *Southwest Social Science Quarterly*, XLIII (March 1963), 357-66.

Gregory, Horace. "Guns of the Roaring West." *Avon Book of Modern Writing No. 2.* New York, 1954, 217-35.

Gruber, Frank. "The Basic Western Novel Plots." *Writer's Year Book,* 1955, 49-53, 160.

Gruber, Frank. *The Pulp Jungle.* Los Angeles: Sherbourne Press, 1967.

Gruber, Frank. "The 7 Ways to Plot a Western." *TV Guide,* VI (August 30, 1958), 5-7.

Homans, Peter. "Puritanism Revisited: An Analysis of the Contemporary Screen-Image Western." *Studies in Public Communication,* III (1961), 73-84.

Hutchinson, W. H. "Grassfire on the Great Plains." *Southwest Review,* XLI (Spring 1956), 181-5.

Hutchinson, W. H. "Virgins, Villains, and Varmints." *Huntington Library Quarterly,* XVI (August 1953), 381-92.

Hutchinson, W. H. "The 'Western Story' as Literature." *Western Humanities Review,* III (January 1949), 33-7.

Jones, Daryl E. "Blood'n Thunder: Virgins, Villains, and Violence in the Dime Novel Western." *Journal of Popular Culture,* IV (Fall 1970), 507-17.

Kitses, Jim. *Horizons West: Studies in Authorship in the Western Film.* Bloomington: Indiana University Press, 1970.

Knauth, Percy. "Gene Autry, Inc." *Life,* XXIV (June 28, 1948), 89-100.

Lahue, Kalton C. *Winners of the Western: The Sagebrush Heroes of the Silent Screen.* South Brunswick: A. S. Barnes, 1970.

Leab, D. J. "The Western Rides Again." *Columbia University Forum,* VII (Summer 1964), 27-30.

Leach, Joseph. "The Paper-Back Texan: Father of the American Western Hero." *Western Humanities Review,* XI (Summer 1957), 267-76.

Mann, E. B. "Southwestern Books." *New Mexico Quarterly,* XXII (Spring 1952), 104-11.

Miller, Alexander. "The 'Western'—A Theological Note." *Christian Century,* LXXIV (November 1957), 1409-10.

Munden, Kenneth J., M.D. "A Contribution to the Psychological Understanding of the Cowboy and His Myth." *American Imago,* XV (Summer 1958), 103-48.

Nussbaum, Martin. "The 'Adult Western' as an American Art Form" *Folklore,* LXX (September 1959), 460-7.

Nussbaum, Martin. "Sociological Symbolism of the Adult Western." *Social Forces,* XXXIX (October 1960), 25-8.

Peverly, Carlos Francis. "The Cowboy in American Literature, 1853-1912." Unpublished master's Thesis, University of Colorado, 1946.

Nye, Russel. *The Unembarrassed Muse: The Popular Arts in America*. New York: The Dial Press, 1970, 280-304. The best account of the rise of the Western.

Percy, Walker. "Decline of the Western." *Commonweal*, LXVIII (May 16, 1958), 181-3.

Reynolds, Quentin. *The Fiction Factory*. New York: Random House, 1955.

Rosenberg, B. "The Poor, Lonesome, Unreviewed Cowboy." *Library Journal*, XXXV (December 15, 1960), 4432-3.

The Roundup. The monthly publication of the Western Writers of America. Each issue contains useful information on the Western.

Rowland, Howard S. "Using the TV Western." *English Journal*, LII (December 1963), 693-6.

Schein, Harry. "The Olympian Cowboy." *The American Scholar*, XXIV (Summer 1955), 309-20.

Sharnik, John "It's Go Western for Young Men." *New York Times Magazine*, (September 24, 1950), 16-22.

Sisk, J. P. "The Western Hero." *Commonwealth*, LXVI (July 12, 1957), 367-9.

"The Six-Gun Galahad." *Time*, LXXIII (March 30, 1959), 52-60.

Smith, Henry Nash. *Virgin Land*. Cambridge: Harvard University Press, 1950.

Sonnichsen, C. L. "The Wyatt Earp Syndrome." *The American West*, VII (May 1970), 26-8, 60-2.

Steckmesser, Ladd. "The Structure and Psychology of the 'Western' Novel." Unpublished master's thesis, University of Iowa, 1956.

Steckmesser, Kent Ladd. *The Western Hero in History and Legend*. Norman: University of Oklahoma Press, 1965.

Straight, Michael. "Truth and Formula for the Western Novel." *South Dakota Review*, II (Autumn 1964), 88-93.

Thompson, Thomas. "Strong, Silent and Stupid." *The Writer*, LXVI (September 1953), 305-6.

Turner, William. "Notes on Western Fiction." *The Roundup*, XVI (February 1968), 1-4; XVII (September 1969), 1-2.

Walker, Don D. "Wister, Roosevelt, and James: A Note on the Western." *American Quarterly*, XII (Fall 1960), 358-66.

Warshow, Robert. "Movie Chronicle: The Westerner." *Partisan Review*, XXI (March-April 1954), 190-203.

White, Trentwell Mason. *How to Write for a Living*. Reynal, 1937, pp. 106-11, 305-9.

Willett, Ralph. "The American Western: Myth and Anti-Myth." *Journal of Popular Culture*, IV (Fall 1970), 455-63.

Wisner, Linda. "The Film Western—Horse Opera or History." Unpublished master's thesis, University of Texas, 1970.

Wylder, Delbert E. "The Popular Western Novel: An Essay Review." *Western American Literature*, IV (Winter 1970), 299-303.
Young, Vernon. "The West in Celluloid, Hollywood's Last Horizons." *Southwest Review*, XXXVIII (Spring 1953), 126-34.

WORKS ON INDIVIDUAL AUTHORS

EDWARD ABBEY

Wylder, Delbert E. "Edward Abbey and the 'Power Elite.' " *Western Review*, VI (Winter 1969), 18-22.

ANDY ADAMS

"Autobiographical Sketch of Andy Adams." *The Junior Book of Authors*, ed. Stanley J. Kunitz and Howard Haycraft. New York: H. W. Wilson Co., 1935, 3-4.

Brunvand, Jan H. "The Hat-in-Mud Tale." *The Sunny Slopes of Long Ago*. Texas Folklore Society Publications, XXXIII, ed. Wilson M. Hudson and Allen Maxwell. Dallas: Southern Methodist University Press, 1966.

Brunvand, Jan H. " 'Sailors' and 'Cowboys' Folklore in Two Popular Classics." *Southern Folklore Quarterly*, XXIX (December 1965), 266-83.

Capps, Benjamin. "A Critical Look at a Classic Western Novel." *Roundup*, XII (June 1964), 2, 4.

Davidson, Levette J. "The Unpublished Manuscripts of Andy Adams." *Colorado Magazine*, XXVIII (April 1951), 97-107.

Dobie, J. Frank. "Andy Adams, Cowboy Chronicler." *Southwest Review*, XI (January 1926), 92-101.

Hudson, Wilson M. *Andy Adams: His Life and Writings*. Dallas: Southern Methodist University Press, 1964.

Hudson, Wilson M. *Andy Adams, Storyteller and Novelist of the Great Plains*. Southwest Writers Series, No. 4. Austin: Steck-Vaughn Company, 1967.

Hudson, William M., ed. *Why the Chisholm Trail Forks and Other Tales of the Cattle Country*. Austin: University of Texas Press, 1956, xi-xxxi.

Molen, Dayle H. "Andy Adams: Classic Novelist of the Western Cattle Drive." *Montana: The Magazine of Western History*, XIX (January 1969), 24-35.

Taylor, Archer. "Americanisms in *The Log of the Cowboy.*" *Western Folklore*, XVIII (January 1959), 39-41.

BESS STREETER ALDRICH

Meier, A. Mabel. "Bess Streeter Aldrich: A Literary Portrait." *Nebraska History*, L (Spring 1969), 67-100.

HENRY WILSON ALLEN

See Will Henry

BROTHER ANTONINUS

See William Everson

JESSIE APPLEGATE

Frear, Samuel Thomas. "Jessie Applegate: An Appraisal of an Uncommon Pioneer." Unpublished master's thesis, University of Oregon, 1961.

GERTRUDE ATHERTON

Forman, H. J. "A Brilliant California Novelist." *California Historical Society Quarterly*, XL (March 1961), 1-10.

McElderry, Bruce R. "Gertrude Atherton and Henry James." *Colby Library Quarterly*, III (November 1954), 269-72.

Underwood, John Curtis. *Literature and Insurgency: Ten Studies in Racial Evolution.* New York: Mitchell Kennerley, 1914, 391-446.

MARY AUSTIN

Austin, Mary. *Earth Horizon: An Autobiography.* Boston: Houghton Mifflin Company, 1932.

Berry, J. Wilkes. "Mary Hunter Austin." *American Literary Realism 1870-1910*, II (Summer 1969), 125-31.

Doyle, Helen McKnight. *Mary Austin: Woman of Genius.* New York: Gotham House, 1939.

Dubois, Arthur E. "Mary Hunter Austin, 1868-1934." *Southwest Review,* XX (April 1935), 231-64.

Ford, Thomas W. *"The American Rhythm:* Mary Austin's Poetic Principle." *Western American Literature,* V (Spring 1970), 3-14.

Gaer, Joseph. *Mary Austin, Bibliography and Biographical Data.* Berkeley: Library Research Digest, Monograph No. 2, 1934.

Lyday, Jo W. *Mary Austin: The Southwest Works.* Southwest Writers Series, No. 16. Austin, Texas: Steck-Vaughn Company, 1968.

Mary Austin: A Memorial. Edited by Willard Houghland. Santa Fe: Laboratory of Anthropology, 1944.

McClanahan, Muriel H. "Aspects of Southwestern Regionalism in the Prose Work of Mary Hunter Austin." Unpublished doctoral dissertation, University of Pittsburgh, 1940.

Pearce, T. M. *The Beloved House.* Caldwell, Idaho: The Caxton Printers, Ltd., 1940.

Pearce, T. M. "Mary Austin and the Patterns of New Mexico." *Southwest Review,* XXII (January 1937), 140-8.

Pearce, T. M. *Mary Hunter Austin.* New York: Twayne, 1965.

Powell, Lawrence Clark. "A Dedication to the Memory of Mary Hunter Austin, 1868-1934." *Arizona and the West,* X (Spring 1968), 1-4.

Ringler, Donald P. *Mary Austin: Kern County Days.* Bakersfield, California: Bear Mountain Books, 1963. The article first appeared in *Southern California Quarterly,* XLV (March 1963), 25-63.

Smith, Henry. "The Feel of the Purposeful Earth." *New Mexico Quarterly,* I (February 1931), 17-33.

Steffens, Lincoln. "Mary Austin and the Desert: A Portrait." *American Mercury,* LXXII (June 1911), 244-63.

Thoroughgood, Inez. "Mary Hunter Austin, Interpreter of the Western Scene, 1888-1906." Unpublished master's thesis, University of California at Los Angeles, 1950.

Van Doren, Carl. "The American Rhythm: Mary Austin, Discoverer and Prophet." *Century Magazine,* CVII (November 1923), 151-6.

Wagenknecht, Edward. "Mary Austin, Sybil." *Cavalcade of the American Novel.* New York: Henry Holt and Co., 1952, 230-5.

Wynn, Dudley. "A Critical Study of the Writings of Mary Hunter Austin, 1868-1934." Unpublished doctoral dissertation, New York University, 1940.

Wynn, Dudley. "Mary Austin, Woman Alone." *Virginia Quarterly Review,* XIII (April 1937), 243-56.

Young, Vernon. "Mary Austin and the Earth Performance." *Southwest Review*, XXXV (Summer 1959), 153-63.

MARGARET JEWETT BAILEY

Nelson, Herbert B. "First True Confession Story Pictures Oregon 'Moral.' " *Oregon Historical Quarterly*, XLV (1944), 168-76.
Nelson, Herbert B. *The Literary Impulse in Pioneer Oregon.* Corvallis: Oregon State University Press, 1948, 36-41.
Nelson, Herbert B. "Ruth Rover's Cup of Sorrow." *Pacific Northwest Quarterly*, L (July 1959), 91-8.

FREDERIC HOMER BALCH

Ballou, Robert. *Early Klickitat Valley Days.* Goldendale, Washington, 1938, 433-43.
Coon, Dela M. "Frederic Homer Balch." *Washington Historical Quarterly*, XV (January 1924), 32-43.
Powers, Alfred. *History of Oregon Literature.* Portland: Metropolitan Press, 1935, 317-32.
Wiley, Leonard. *The Granite Boulder: A Biography of Frederic Homer Balch.* Portland, Oregon: n.p., 1970.

S. OMAR BARKER

Dewey, Evelyn G. "S. Omar Barker: Man of the Southwest." Unpublished master's thesis, Eastern New Mexico University, 1954.

ROY BEDICHEK

Bedichek, Roy. "My Father and Then My Mother." *Southwest Review*, LII (1967), 324-42.
Dugger, Ronnie, ed. *Three Men in Texas: Bedichek, Webb, and Dobie.* Austin: University of Texas Press, 1967.
James, Eleanor. *Roy Bedichek.* Southwest Writers Series, No. 32. Austin, Texas: Steck-Vaughn Company, 1970.
Owens, William A. *Three Friends: Bedichek, Dobie, Webb.* Garden City, New York: Doubleday & Company Inc., 1969.

EMERSON BENNETT - SIDNEY MOSS

Mills, Randall V. "Emerson Bennett's Two Oregon Novels." *Oregon Historical Quarterly*, XLI (1940), 367-81.
Nelson, Herbert B. *The Literary Impulse in Pioneer Oregon.* Corvallis: Oregon State University Press, 1948, 44-51.
Powers, Alfred. *History of Oregon Literature.* Portland: Metropolitan Press, 1935, 195-203.

THOMAS BERGER

Dippie, Brian W. "Jack Crabb and the Sole Survivors of Custer's Last Stand." *Western American Literature*, IV (Fall 1969), 189-202.
Gurian, Jay. "Style in the Literary Desert: *Little Big Man.*" *Western American Literature*, III (Winter 1969), 285-96.
Lee, L. L. "American, Western, Picaresque: Thomas Berger's *Little Big Man.*" *South Dakota Review*, IV (Summer 1966), 35-42.
Turner, Frederick W. III. "Melville and Thomas Berger: The Novelist as Cultural Anthropologist." *The Centennial Review*, XIII (Winter 1969), 101-21.
Wylder, Delbert E. "Thomas Berger's *Little Big Man* as Literature." *Western American Literature*, III (Winter 1969), 273-84.

DON BERRY

Porter, Kenneth. "Northwest Writer Emerges." *Northwest Review*, III (Summer 1960), 98-101.

AMBROSE BIERCE

Bahr, H. W. "Ambrose Bierce and Realism." *Southern Quarterly*, I (July 1963), 309-33.
Fatout, Paul. "Ambrose Bierce (1842-1914)." *American Literary Realism 1870-1910*, I (Fall 1967), 13-9.
Fatout, Paul. *Ambrose Bierce and the Black Hills.* Norman: University of Oklahoma Press, 1956.
Fatout, Paul. *Ambrose Bierce: The Devil's Lexicographer.* Norman: University of Oklahoma Press, 1951.
Fortenberry, George E., comp. and ed. "Ambrose Bierce (1841-1914): A Critical Bibliography of Secondary Comment." *American Literary Realism 1870-1910*, IV (Winter 1971), 11-56.

Gaer, Joseph, editor. *Ambrose Gwinett Bierce: Bibliography and Biographical Data.* Berkely, 1935; New York: Burt Franklin, 1968.

Goldstein, J. S. "Edwin Markham, Ambrose Bierce, and 'The Man with the Hoe.' " *Modern Language Notes,* LXIX (March 1943), 165-75.

Grattan, C. Hartley. *Bitter Bierce: A Mystery of American Life.* New York: Doubleday, Doran and Company, 1929.

Grenander, M. E. "Ambrose Bierce, John Camden Hutten, *The Fiend's Delight,* and *Nuggets and Dust." Huntington Library Quarterly,* XXVIII (August 1965), 353-71.

Grenander, M. E. "Bierce's Turn of the Screw." *Western Humanities Review,* XI (Summer 1957), 257-64.

Klein, Marcus. "San Francisco and Her Hateful Ambrose Bierce." *Hudson Review,* VII (August 1954), 392-407.

Loveman, S. ed. *Twenty-one Letters of Ambrose Bierce.* Cleveland, 1922.

McWilliams, Carey. "Ambrose Bierce." *American Mercury,* XVI (February 1929), 215-22.

McWilliams, Carey. *Ambrose Bierce: A Biography.* New York: A. C. Boni, 1929; Archon Books, 1967.

McWilliams, Carey. "The Mystery of Ambrose Bierce." *American Mercury,* XXII (May 1945), 330-7.

Neale, Walter. *Life of Ambrose Bierce.* New York: Walter Neale, Publisher, 1929; New York: AMS Press, 1969.

O'Connor, Richard. *Ambrose Bierce: A Biography.* Boston: Little, Brown and Co., 1967.

Pope, Bertha, ed. *The Letters of Ambrose Bierce.* San Francisco: Book Club of California, 1922.

Starrett, Vincent. *Ambrose Bierce.* Chicago: Walter M. Hill, 1920.

Starrett, Vincent. *A Bibliography of the Writings of Ambrose Bierce.* Philadelphia: The Centaur Book Shop, 1929.

Wiggins, Robert A. *Ambrose Bierce.* Minneapolis: University of Minnesota Press, 1964.

Wiggins, Robert A. "Ambrose Bierce: A Romantic in an Age of Realism." *American Literary Realism 1870-1910,* IV (Winter 1971), 1-10.

Woodruff, Stuart C. *The Short Stories of Ambrose Bierce: A Study in Polarity.* Pittsburgh: University of Pittsburgh Press, 1964.

ROBERT BLY

Hertzel, Leo J. "What About Writers in the North?" *South Dakota Review,* V (Spring 1967), 3-19.

Heyen, William. "Inward to the World: The Poetry of Robert Bly."
The Far Point, III (1969), 42-50.

Janssens, G. A. M. "The Present State of American Poetry: Robert
Bly and James Wright." *English Studies*, LI (April 1970), 112-
37.

Piccione, Anthony. "Robert Bly and the Deep Image." Unpublished
doctoral dissertation, Ohio University, 1969.

Steele, Frank. "Three Questions Answered." *Tennessee Poetry
Journal*, II (1969), 23-8.

B. M. BOWER
(Bertha Sinclair)

Nye, Russel. *The Unembarrassed Muse: The Popular Arts in
America*. New York: The Dial Press, 291-2.

West, Gordon. "Remember 'Chip of the Flying U'?" *True West*, XX
(September-October 1971), 31.

RICHARD BRADFORD

Etulain, Richard W. "Richard Bradford's *Red Sky at Morning:* New
Novel of the Southwest." *Western Review*, VIII(Spring 1971), 57-
62.

MAX BRAND
(Frederick Faust)

Easton, Robert. *Max Brand: The Big "Westerner."* Norman:
University of Oklahoma Press, 1970.

Reynolds, Quentin. *The Fiction Factory*. New York: Random House,
1955.

Richardson, Darrell C. *Max Brand: The Man and His Work*. Fantasy
Publishing Company, 1952.

Schoolcraft, John, ed. *The Notebooks and Poems of "Max Brand."*
New York: Dodd, Mead and Company, 1957.

DOROTHY BRETT

Manchester, John. "Thoughts on Brett: 1967." *South Dakota
Review*, V (Summer 1967), 3-9.

Morrill, Claire. "Three Women of Taos: Frieda Lawrence, Mabel Luhan, and Dorothy Brett." *South Dakota Review*, II (Spring 1965), 3-22.

FRANK BRINK

Petersen, Lance. "Alaskan Men of Letters: Frank Brink." *Alaska Review*, I (Spring 1964), 36-9.

CHARLES FARRAR BROWNE
(Artemas Ward)

Austin, James C. *Artemas Ward.* New York: Twayne Publishers, 1964.

Blair, Walter. *Native American Humor.* New York: American Book Company, 1937.

Fatout, Paul. "Artemas Ward Among the Mormons." *Western Humanities Review*, XIV (Spring 1960), 193-9.

Hingston, Edward P. *The Genial Showman.* New York: Harper, 1870.

Jaynes, Bryson L. "Artemas Ward Among the Mormons." *Research Studies of the State College of Washington*, XXV (March 1957), 75-84.

Lorch, Fred W. "Mark Twain's 'Artemas Ward' Lecture on the Tour of 1871-1872." *New England Quarterly*, XXV (1952), 327-43.

McKee Irving. "Artemas Ward in California and Nevada, 1863-1864." *Pacific Historical Review*, XX (February 1951), 11-23.

Nock, A. J. "Artemas Ward's America." *Atlantic Monthly*, CLIV (September 1934), 273-81.

Reed, John Q. "Artemas Ward: A Critical Study." Unpublished doctoral dissertation, State University of Iowa, 1955.

Seitz, Don C. *Artemas Ward (Charles Farrar Browne): A Biography and Bibliography.* New York: Harper and Brothers, 1919.

Williams, Stanley T. "Artemas the Delicious." *Virginia Quarterly Review*, XXVIII (Spring 1952), 214-27.

Wright, William. "Artemas Ward in Nevada." *California Illustrated Magazine*, IV (August 1893), 403-5.

J. ROSS BROWNE

Browne, Lina Fergusson, ed. *J. Ross Browne: His Letters, Journals and Writings.* Albuquerque: University of New Mexico Press, 1969.

Browne, Lina Fergusson, ed. "J. Ross Browne in the Apache Country." *New Mexico Quarterly,* XXXV (Spring 1965), 5-28.

Dillon, Richard H. "J. Ross Browne and the Corruptible West." *The American West,* II (Spring 1965), 37-45.

Dillon, Richard H. *J. Ross Browne, Confidential Agent in Old California.* Norman: University of Oklahoma Press, 1965.

Rock, Francis John. *J. Ross Browne: A Biography.* Washington, D.C.: Catholic University of America, 1929.

WITTER BYNNER

Lindsay, Robert O. *Witter Bynner: A Bibliography.* Albuquerque: University of New Mexico, 1967.

ROBERT CANTWELL

Bowman, John Scott. "The Proletarian Novel in America." Unpublished doctoral dissertation, Pennsylvania State College, 1939.

Conroy, Jack. "Robert Cantwell's 'Land of Plenty.' " in *Proletarian Writers of the Thirties,* ed. David Madden. Carbondale: Southern Illinois Press, 1968. 74-84.

Rideout, Walter B. *The Radical Novel in the United States.* Cambridge: Harvard University Press, 1956, 174-8 ff.

BENJAMIN CAPPS

Etulain, Richard W. *"The White Man's Road:* An Appreciation." *Southwestern American Literature,* I (May 1971), 88-92.

Sonnichsen, C. L. "The New Style Western." *South Dakota Review,* IV (Summer 1966), 22-8.

ROBERT ORMAND CASE

Newton, Dwight B. "Meet Robert Ormand Case." *The Roundup,* IV (March 1956), 3-4.

WILLA CATHER

Auchincloss, Louis. *Pioneers and Caretakers: A Study of Nine Women Novelists.* Minneapolis: University of Minnesota Press, 1965.

Baker, Bruce II. "Nebraska Regionalism in Selected Works of Willa Cather." *Western American Literature,* III (Spring 1968), 19-35.

Baum, Bernard. "Willa Cather's Waste Land." *South Atlantic Quarterly,* XLVIII (October 1949), 589-601.

Bennett, Mildred R. *The World of Willa Cather.* New York: Dodd, Mead & Co., 1951; Lincoln: University of Nebraska Press, 1961.

Bloom, Edward A. and Lillian D. "The Genesis of *Death Come for the Archbishop." American Literature,* XXVI (January 1955), 476-506.

Bloom, Edward, and Lillian Bloom. *Willa Cather's Gift of Sympathy.* Carbondale: Southern Illinois University Press, 1962.

Bloom, Edward A., and Lillian D. "Willa Cather's Novels of the Frontier: A Study in Thematic Symbolism." *American Literature,* XXI (March 1949), 71-93.

Bloom, Edward A. and Lillian D. "Willa Cather's Novels of the Frontier: The Symbolic Function of 'Machine-Made Materialism.' " *University of Toronto Quarterly,* XX (October 1950), 45-60.

Bonham, Barbara. *Willa Cather.* Chilton Books, 1970.

Bradford, Curtis. "Willa Cather's Uncollected Short Stories." *American Literature,* XXVI (January 1955), 537-51.

Brennan, Joseph X. "Music and Willa Cather." *The University Review,* XXXI (June 1965), 257-64.

Brennan, Joseph X. "Willa Cather and Music." *The University Review,* XXXI (March 1965), 175-83.

Brown, E. K. "Homage to Willa Cather." *Yale Review,* XXXVI (1946), 77-92.

Brown, E. K. "Willa Cather and the West." *University of Toronto Quarterly,* V (July 1936), 544-66.

Brown, Edward K. *Willa Cather: A Critical Biography.* New York: Alfred A. Knopf, 1953. Completed by Leon Edel.

Charles, Sister Peter Damian, O. P. "Death Comes for the Archbishop: A Novel of Love and Death." *New Mexico Quarterly,* XXXVI (Winter 1966-67), 389-403.

Charles, Sister Peter Damian, O. P. "Love and Death in the Novels of Willa Cather." Unpublished doctoral dissertation, University of Notre Dame, 1965.

Charles, Sister Peter Damian, O. P. "My Ántonia: A Dark Dimension." *Western American Literature,* II (Summer 1967), 91-108.

Curtin, William M., ed. *The World and the Parish: Willa Cather's Articles and Reviews, 1893-1902.* 2 vols. Lincoln: University of Nebraska Press, 1970.

Dahl, Curtis. "An American *Georgic:* Willa Cather's *My Ántonia.*" *Comparative Literature,* VII (Winter 1955), 43-51.

Daiches, David. *Willa Cather: A Critical Introduction.* Ithaca: Cornell University Press, 1951; New York: Collier, 1962.

Feger, Lois. "The Dark Dimension of Willa Cather's *My Ántonia.*" *English Journal,* LIX (September 1970), 774-9.

Ferguson, J. M., Jr. " 'Vague Outlines': Willa Cather's Enchanted Bluffs." *Western Review,* VII (Spring 1970), 61-4.

Finestone, Harry. "Willa Cather's Apprenticeship." Unpublished doctoral dissertation, University of Chicago, 1953.

Footman, Robert H. "The Genius of Willa Cather." *American Literature,* X (1938), 123-41.

Forman, H. J. "Willa Cather: A Voice from the Prairie." *Southwest Review,* XLVII (Summer 1962), 248-58.

Fox, Maynard. "Proponents of Order: Tom Outland and Bishop Latour." *Western American Literature,* IV (Summer 1969), 107-15.

Gale, Robert. "Willa Cather and the Usable Past." *Nebraska History,* XLII (September 1961), 181-90.

Geismar, Maxwell. "Willa Cather: Lady in the Wilderness." in *The Last of the Provincials: The American Novel, 1915-1925.* Boston: Houghton Mifflin Company, 1947, 153-220.

Giannone, Richard. *Music in Willa Cather's Fiction.* Lincoln: University of Nebraska Press, 1968.

Helmick, Evelyn Thomas. "Myth in the Works of Willa Cather." *Midcontinent American Studies Journal,* IX (Fall 1968), 63-9.

Hicks, Granville. "The Case Against Willa Cather." *English Journal,* XXII (1933), 703-10.

Hutchinson, Phyllis Martin. "The Writings of Willa Cather: A List of Works by and about Her." *Bulletin of the New York Library,* LX (June 1956), 267-87; (July 1956), 338-56; (August 1956), 378-400.

Jacks, L. V. "Willa Cather and the Southwest." *New Mexico Quarterly,* XXVII (Spring-Summer 1957), 83-7.

Keeler, Clinton. "Narrative Without Accent: Willa Cather and Puvis de Chavannes." *American Quarterly,* XVII (Spring 1965), 119-26.

La Hood, Marvin. "Conrad Richter and Willa Cather: Some Similarities." *Xavier University Studies,* IX (Spring 1970), 33-44.

Lambert, Maude Eugenie. "Theme and Craftsmanship in Willa Cather's Novels." Unpublished doctoral dissertation, University of North Carolina, 1965.

Lee, Robert Edson. *From East to West.* Urbana: University of Illinois Press, 112-35.

Lewis, Edith. *Willa Cather Living: A Personal Record.* New York: Alfred A. Knopf, 1953.

Martin, Terence. "The Drama of Memory in *My Antonia.*" *PMLA*, LXXXIV (March 1969), 304-11.

Miller, James E., Jr. *"My Antonia:* A Frontier Drama of Time." *American Quarterly*, X (Winter 1958), 476-84.

Miller, James E., Jr. "The Nebraska Encounter: Willa Cather and Wright Morris." *Prairie Schooner*, XLI (Summer 1967), 165-7.

Randall, John H. *The Landscape and the Looking Glass: Willa Cather's Search for Value.* Boston: Houghton Mifflin Company, 1960.

Randall, John H. "Willa Cather: The Middle West Revisited." *New Mexico Quarterly*, XXXI (Spring 1961), 25-36.

Reaver, J. Russell. "Mythic Motivation in Willa Cather's *O Pioneers!"* *Western Folklore*, XXVII (January 1968), 19-25.

Schneider, Sister Lucy, C. S. J. "Cather's 'Land Philosophy' in *Death Comes for the Archbishop."* *Renascence*, XXII (Winter 1970), 78-86.

Schneider, Sister Lucy. "Willa Cather's Early Stories in Light of Her 'Land Philosophy.' " *The Midwest Quarterly*, IX (August 1967), 75-93.

Schroeter, James Marvin. *Willa Cather and Her Critics.* Ithaca, New York: Cornell University Press, 1967.

Seibel, George. "Miss Willa Cather from Nebraska." *New Colophon*, II (September 1949), 195-208.

Sergeant, Elizabeth Shepley. *Willa Cather: A Memoir.* Philadelphia: Lippincott, 1953; Lincoln: University of Nebraska Press, 1963.

Shively, James R. ed. *Writings from Willa Cather's Campus Years.* Lincoln: University of Nebraska Press, 1950.

Slote, Bernice, ed. *The Kingdom of Art: Willa Cather's First Principles and Critical Statements, 1893-1896.* Lincoln: University of Nebraska Press. 1967.

Slote, Bernice. "Willa Cather," in *Fifteen Modern American Authors*, edited by Jackson R. Bryer. Durham: Duke University Press, 1969, 23-62.

Slote, Bernice. "Willa Cather as a Regional Writer." *Kansas Quarterly*, II (Spring 1970), 7-15.

Stegner, Wallace. "Willa Cather, *My Ántonia."* *The American Novel from James Fenimore Cooper to William Faulkner*, ed. Wallace Stegner. New York: Basic Books, 1965.

Stegner, Wallace. "The West Authentic: Willa Cather." *The Sound of Mountain Water.* Garden City: Doubleday and Company, 1969, 237-49.

Stewart, D. H. "Cather's Mortal Comedy." *Queen's Quarterly,* LXXIII (Summer 1966), 244-59.

Toler, Sister Colette. "Man as Creator of Art and Civilization in the Works of Willa Cather." Unpublished doctoral dissertation, University of Notre Dame, 1965.

Van Ghent, Dorothy. *Willa Cather.* Minneapolis: University of Minnesota Press, 1964.

Wagenknecht, Edward. "Willa Cather." *Sewanee Review,* XXXVII (1929), 221-39.

Walker, Don D. "The Western Humanism of Willa Cather." *Western American Literature,* I (Summer 1966), 75-90.

Whittington, Curtis, Jr. " 'The Stream and the Broken Pottery': The Form of Willa Cather's *Death Comes for the Archbishop.*" *McNeese Review,* XVI (1965), 16-24.

Woodress, James. *Willa Cather: Her Life and Art.* New York: Pegasus, 1970.

Woodress, James. "Willa Cather Seen Clear." *Papers on Language and Literature,* VII (Winter 1971), 96-109.

J. SMEATON CHASE

Dillon, Richard H. "Prose Poet of the Trail: J. Smeaton Chase." *The Book Club of California Quarterly Newsletter,* XXXV (Spring 1970), 27-36.

WALTER VAN TILBURG CLARK

Andersen, Kenneth. "Character Portrayal in *The Ox-Bow Incident.*" *Western American Literature,* IV (Winter 1970) 287-98.

Andersen, Kenneth. "Form in Walter Van Tilburg Clark's *The Ox-Bow Incident.*" *Western Review,* VI (Spring 1969), 19-25.

Bates, Barclay W. "Clark's Man for All Seasons: The Achievement of Wholeness in *The Ox-Bow Incident.*" *Western American Literature,* III (Spring 1968), 37-49.

Bluestone, George. *Novels into Film.* Baltimore: The Johns Hopkins Press, 1957, 170-96.

Boardman, Arthur. "The Muted Horn: A Study of the Prose of Walter Van Tilburg Clark." Unpublished master's thesis, University of Nevada, 1953.

Carpenter, Frederic I. "The West of Walter Van Tilburg Clark." *College English,* XIII (February 1952), 243-8.

Christian, Aubry D. "Nature and Dream: The Symbolic Mode of Walter Van Tilburg Clark." Unpublished master's thesis, University of Texas, 1965.

Cochran, Robert W. "Nature and the Nature of Man in *The Ox-Bow Incident.*" *Western American Literature*, V (Winter 1971), 253-64.

Cohen, Edward H. "Clark's 'The Portable Phonograph.' " *Explicator*, XXVIII (April 1970), 69.

Eisinger, Chester E. *Fiction of the Forties*. Chicago: University of Chicago Press, 1963, 310-24.

Eisinger, Chester E. "The Fiction of Walter Van Tilburg Clark: Man and Nature in the West." *Southwest Review*, XLIV (Summer 1959), 214-26.

Etulain, Richard. "Walter Van Tilburg Clark: A Bibliography." *South Dakota Review*, III(Autumn 1965), 73-7.

Folsom, James K. *The American Western Novel*. New Haven: College and University Press, 1966, 172-6.

Gurian, Jay. "The Unwritten West." *The American West*, II (Winter 1965), 59-63.

Herrmann, John. "The Death of the Artist as Hero." *South Dakota Review*, IV (Summer 1966), 51-5.

Houghton, Donald E. "The Failure of Speech in *The Ox-Bow Incident.*" *English Journal*, LIX (December 1970), 1245-51.

Houghton, Donald E. "Man and Animals in 'The Indian Well.' " *Western American Literature*, VI (Fall 1971), 215-8.

Kuehl, John R. "Walter Van Tilburg Clark: A Bibliography," *Bulletin of Bibliography*, XXII (September-December 1956), 18-20.

Lee, L. L. "Walter Van Tilburg Clark's Ambiguous American Dream." *College English*, XXVI (February 1965) 382-7.

LeRoy, Robert Orrelle. "A Study of the Works of Walter Van Tilburg Clark." Unpublished master's thesis, University of Wyoming, 1952.

Malloy, Jean Norris. "The World of Walter Van Tilburg Clark." Unpublished doctoral dissertation, Northwestern University, 1968.

Milton, John R. "The American Novel: The Search for Home, Tradition, and Identity." *Western Humanities Review*, XVI (Spring 1962), 169-80.

Milton, John R. "Conversation with Walter Van Tilburg Clark." *South Dakota Review*, IX (Spring 1971), 27-38.

Milton, John R. "The Western Attitude: Walter Van Tilburg Clark." *Critique*, II (Winter 1959), 57-73.

Portz, John. "Idea and Symbol in Walter Van Tilburg Clark." *Accent*, XVII (Spring 1957), 112-28.

Powell, William D. "Walter Van Tilburg Clark and *The Watchful Gods.*" Unpublished master's thesis, New Mexico Highlands University, 1965.

Stein, Paul. "Cowboys and Unicorns: The Novels of Walter Van Tilburg Clark." *Western American Literature,* V (Winter 1971), 265-75.

Swallow, Alan. "The Mavericks." *Critique,* II (Winter 1959), 84-8.

West, Ray B. Jr. "The Use of Setting in 'The Wind and the Snow of Winter'." *The Art of Writing Fiction.* New York: Thomas Y. Crowell Company, 1968, 181-7.

Westbrook, Max. "The Archetypal Ethic of *The Ox-Bow Incident.*" *Western American Literature,* I (Summer 1966), 105-18.

Westbrook, Max. "Internal Debate as Discipline: Clark's *The Watchful Gods.*" *Western American Literature,* I (Fall 1966), 153-65.

Westbrook, Max. *Walter Van Tilburg Clark.* New York: Twayne Publishers, Inc., 1969.

Wilner, Herbert. "Walter Van Tilburg Clark," *Western Review* XX (Winter 1956), 103-22.

Young, Vernon. "An American Dream and Its Parody." *Arizona Quarterly,* VI (Summer 1950), 112-23.

Young, Vernon. "God's Without Heroes: The Tentative Myth of Walter Van Tilburg Clark." *Arizona Quarterly,* VII (Summer 1951), 110-9.

WILLIAM CLARK
(Lewis and Clark)

See Meriwether Lewis

SAMUEL CLEMENS
(Mark Twain)

Baender, Paul. "The 'Jumping Frog' as a Comedian's First Virtue." *Modern Philology,* LX (February 1963), 192-200.

Baldanza, Frank. *Mark Twain: An Introduction and Interpretation.* New York: Barnes and Noble, 1961.

Bellamy, Gladys Carmen. *Mark Twain as a Literary Artist.* Norman: University of Oklahoma Press, 1950.

Benson, Ivan. *Mark Twain's Western Years.* Stanford: Stanford University Press, 1938.

Blair, Walter. *Mark Twain and Huck Finn.* Berkeley: University of California Press, 1960.

Blues, Thomas. *Mark Twain and the Community.* Lexington: University Press of Kentucky, 1970.

Branch, Edgar M. "A Chronological Bibliography of the Writings of Samuel Clemens to June 8, 1867." *American Literature,* XVIII (May 1946), 109-59.

Branch, Edgar M., ed. *Clemens of the "Call": Mark Twain in San Francisco.* Berkeley: University of California Press, 1969.

Branch, Edgar Marquess. *The Literary Apprenticeship of Mark Twain.* Urbana: University of Illinois Press, 1950.

Branch, Edgar M. " 'My Voice is still for Setchell': A Background Study of 'Jim Smiley and His Jumping Frog.' " *PMLA,* LXXXII (December 1967), 591-601.

Brashear, Minnie M. *Mark Twain, Son of Missouri.* Chapel Hill: University of North Carolina Press, 1934.

Brooks, Van Wyck. *The Ordeal of Mark Twain.* Rev. ed. New York: E. P. Dutton & Co., 1933.

Budd, Louis J. *Mark Twain: Social Philosopher.* Bloomington: Indiana University Press, 1962.

Burnet, R. A. "Mark Twain in the Northwest—1895." *Pacific Northwest Quarterly,* XLII (July 1951), 187-202.

Camp, James E. and X. J. Kennedy, ed. *Mark Twain's Frontier: A Textbook of Primary Source Materials for Student Research and Writing.* New York: Holt, Rinehart, Winston, 1963.

Canby, Henry Seidel. *Turn West, Turn East.* Boston: Houghton Mifflin Company, 1951.

Carstensen, Vernon. "The West Mark Twain Did Not See." *Pacific Northwest Quarterly,* LV (October 1964), 170-6.

Carter, Paul J., Jr. "The Influence of the Nevada Frontier on Mark Twain." *Western Humanities Review,* XIII (Winter 1959), 61-70.

Clark, Harry Hayden. "Mark Twain." *Eight American Authors,* ed. Floyd Stovall. New York: MLA, 1956; New York: W. W. Norton and Company, 1963.

Covici, Pascal, Jr. *Mark Twain's Humor: The Image of a World.* Dallas: Southern Methodist University Press, 1962.

Cox, James M. *Mark Twain: The Fate of Humor.* Princeton, N.J.: Princeton University Press, 1966.

Cracroft, Richard H. "The Gentle Blasphemer: Mark Twain, Holy Scripture, and the Book of Mormon." *Brigham Young University Studies,* XI (Winter 1971), 119-40.

Cunliffe, Marcus. "American Humor and the Rise of the West: Mark Twain." *The Literature of the United States.* London: Penguin Books, 1954, 151-69.

Dennis, Larry R. "Mark Twain and the Dark Angel." *The Midwest Quarterly,* VIII (January 1967), 181-97.

DeVoto, Bernard. *Mark Twain at Work*. Cambridge, Massachusetts: Harvard University Press, 1942.

DeVoto, Bernard. *Mark Twain's America*. Boston: Little, Brown, 1932.

Duckett, Margaret. *Mark Twain and Bret Harte*. Norman: University of Oklahoma Press, 1964.

Fatout, Paul. *Mark Twain in Virginia City*. Bloomington: Indiana University Press, 1964.

Ferguson, DeLancey. *Mark Twain: Man and Legend*. Indianapolis: Bobbs-Merrill, 1943.

Foner, Philip S. *Mark Twain: Social Critic*. New York: International Publishers, 1958.

Fried, Martin B. "The Composition, Sources, and Popularity of Mark Twain's *Roughing It.*" Unpublished doctroral dissertation, University of Chicago, 1951.

Geismar, Maxwell. *Mark Twain: An American Prophet*. Boston: Houghton Mifflin Company, 1970.

Hill, Hamlin. "Mark Twain and His Enemies." *The Southern Review*, IV (Spring 1968), 520-9.

Howells, William Dean. *My Mark Twain*. New York: Harper, 1910.

Hudson, Ruth. "A Literary 'Area of Freedom' between Irving and Twain." *Western Humanities Review*, XII (Winter 1959), 47-60.

James, G. W. "Mark Twain and the Pacific Coast." *Pacific Monthly*, XXIV (1910), 115-32.

Johnson, Merle. *A Bibliography of the Works of Mark Twain*. Rev. ed. New York: Harper, 1935.

Kaplan, Justin. *Mr. Clemens and Mark Twain: A Biography*. New York: Simon and Schuster, 1966.

Krause, S. J. "The Art and Satire of Twain's 'Jumping Frog' Story." *American Quarterly*, XVI (Winter 1964), 562-76.

Krause, S. J. "Cooper's Literary Offenses: Mark Twain in Wonderland." *New England Quarterly*, XXXVIII (September 1965), 291-311.

Leary, Lewis. *Mark Twain*. Minneapolis: *University of Minnesota Press, 1960*.

Lee, Robert Edson. *From West to East*. Urbana: University of Illinois Press, 1966, 82-111.

Long, E. Hudson. *Mark Twain Handbook*. New York: Hendricks House, 1957.

Loomis, C. Grant. "Dan De Quille's Mark Twain." *Pacific Historical Review*, XV (1946), 336-47.

Lorch, Fred W. "Mark Twain's Lecture for *Roughing It.*" *American Literature*, XXII (1950), 290-307.

Lorch, Fred W. *The Trouble Begins at Eight*. Ames: Iowa State University Press, 1968.

Lynn, Kenneth S. "Huck and Jim." *Yale Review*, XVII (Spring 1958), 421-31.

Lynn, Kenneth S. *Mark Twain and Southwestern Humor*. Boston: Little, Brown, 1959.

Mack, Effie Mona. *Mark Twain in Nevada*. New York: Charles Scribners, 1947.

Marx, Leo. "Mr. Eliot, Mr. Trilling, and *Huckleberry Finn*" American Scholar, XXII (August 1953), 423-40.

Marx, Leo. "The Pilot and the Passenger: Landscape Conventions and the Style of *Huckleberry Finn*." *American Literature*, XXVII (May 1956), 129-46.

Meyer, Harold. "Mark Twain on the Comstock." *Southwest Review*, XII (1927), 197-207.

McKee, John DeWitt. "Roughing It as Retrospective Reporting." *Western American Literature*, V (Summer 1970), 113-9.

Paine, Albert Bigelow. *Mark Twain: A Biography*. 3 vols. New York: Harper, 1912.

Petit, Arthur G. "Mark Twain's Attitude Toward Negro in the West, 1861-1867." *The Western Historical Quarterly*, I (January 1970), 51-62.

Reed, J. Q. "Mark Twain: West Coast Journalist." *Midwest Journal*, I (Winter 1960), 141-61.

Rogers, Franklin, ed. *The Pattern for Mark Twain's Roughing It*. Berkeley: University of California Press, 1961.

Rogers, Franklin R. "The Road to Reality: Burlesque Travel Literature and Mark Twain's *Roughing It*." *Bulletin of the New York Public Library*, LXVII (March 1963), 155-68.

Ryan, Pat. "Mark Twain: Frontier Theatre Critic." *Arizona Quarterly*, XVI (August 1960), 197-209.

Smith, Henry Nash. *Mark Twain: The Development of a Writer*. Cambridge, Massachusetts: Harvard University Press, 1962.

Smith, Henry Nash and Frederick Anderson, eds. *Mark Twain of the Enterprise*. Berkeley: University of California Press, 1957.

Smith, Henry Nash, and William M. Gibson, eds. *Mark Twain-Howells Letters*. 2 vols. Cambridge: Harvard University Press, 1960.

Solomon, Roger B. *Mark Twain and the Image of History*. New Haven: Yale University Press, 1961.

Stone, Albert E., Jr. *The Innocent Eye: Childhood in Mark Twain's Imagination*. New Haven: Yale University Press, 1961.

Taper, Bernard, ed. *Mark Twain's San Francisco*. New York: McGraw-Hill, 1963.

Taylor, J. Golden. "Introduction to 'The Celebrated Jumping Frog of Calaveras County.'" *The American West*, II (Fall 1965), 73-6.

Wagenknecht, Edward. *Mark Twain: The Man and His Work.* Rev. ed. Norman, Oklahoma: University of Oklahoma Press, 1961.
Wecter, Dixon. "Mark Twain and the West." *Huntington Library Quarterly,* VIII (1945), 359-77.
Wecter, Dixon. *Sam Clemens of Hannibal,* ed. Elizabeth Wecter. Boston: Houghton Mifflin, 1952.
West, Ray B., Jr. "Mark Twain's Idyl of Frontier America." *University of Kansas City Review,* XV (1948), 92-104.
Wiggins, Robert A. *Mark Twain: Jackleg Novelist.* Seattle: University of Washington Press, 1964.
Wister, Owen. "In Homage to Mark Twain." *Harper's Magazine,* CLXXI (1935), 547-66.

JAMES FENIMORE COOPER

Baym, Nina. "The Women of Cooper's Leatherstocking Tales." *American Quarterly,* XXIII (December 1971), 696-709.
Beard, James F., ed. *The Letters and Journals of James Fenimore Cooper.* 6 vols. Cambridge: Harvard University Press, 1960—.
Beard, James Franklin. "James Fenimore Cooper." *Fifteen American Authors Before 1900: Bibliographic Essays on Research and Criticism.* Madison: University of Wisconsin Press, 1971.
Bewley, Marius. *The Eccentric Design.* New York: Columbia University Press, 1959, 47-100.
Bewley, Marius. "The Cage and the Prairie: Two Notes on Symbolism." *Hudson Review,* X (Autumn 1957), 408-13.
Bier, Jesse. "Lapsarians on *The Prairie:* Cooper's Novel." *Texas Studies in Literature and Language,* IV (Spring 1962), 49-57.
Boynton, Henry W. *James Fenimore Cooper.* New York: Appleton-Century, 1931.
Chase, Richard. *The American Novel and Its Tradition.* Garden City: Doubleday, 1957, 52-65.
Clavel, Marcel. *Fenimore Cooper and His Critics.* Aix-en-Provence: Imprimerie Universitaire de Provence, 1938.
Cunningham, Mary, ed. *James Fenimore Cooper: A Re-Appraisal.* Cooperstown, N.Y.: New York State Historical Association, 1954.
Dekker, George. *James Fenimore Cooper: The Novelist.* London: Routledge and Kegan Paul, 1967.
Flanagan, John T. "The Authenticity of Cooper's *The Prairie.*" *Modern Language Quarterly,* II (March 1941), 99-104.
Frederick, John T. "Cooper's Eloquent Indians." *PMLA,* LXXXI (1956), 1004-17.

Fussell, Edwin. *Frontier: American Literature and the American West.* Princeton: Princeton University Press, 1965, pp. 27-68.

Grossman, James. *James Fenimore Cooper.* New York: William Sloane, 1949.

House, Kay Seymour. *Cooper's Americans.* Columbus: Ohio State University Press, 1965.

Jones, Howard Mumford. *The Frontier in American Fiction.* Jerusalem, 1926, 26-50.

Kaul, A. N. *The American Vision: Actual and Ideal In Nineteenth Century Fiction.* New Haven: Yale University Press, 1963, 84-138.

Lawrence, D. H. *Studies in Classic American Literature.* New York: Thomas Seltzer, 1923, 50-92.

Lewis, Merrill. "Lost—and Found—in the Wilderness: The Desert Metaphor in Cooper's *The Prairie." Western American Literature,* V (Fall 1970), 195-204.

Lounsbury, Thomas R. *James Fenimore Cooper.* Boston: Houghton Mifflin Company, 1882.

Mills, Gordon. "The Symbolic Wilderness: James Fenimore Cooper and Jack London." *Nineteenth-Century Fiction,* XIII (1959), 329-40.

Muszynska-Wallace, E. Soteris. "The Sources of *The Prairie." American Literature,* XXI (May 1949), 191-200.

Noble, David W. "Cooper, Leatherstocking and the Death of the American Adam." *American Quarterly,* XVI (Fall 1964), 419-31.

Paine, Gregory. "The Indians of *The Leatherstocking Tales." Studies in Philology,* XXIII (1926), 16-39.

Pearce, Roy Harvey. "The Leatherstocking Tales Re-examined." *South Atlantic Quarterly,* XLVI (October 1947), 524-36.

Pound, Louise. "The Dialect of Cooper's Leatherstocking." *American Speech,* II(1927), 479-88.

Ringe, Donald A. *James Fenimore Cooper,* New York: Twayne 1962.

Ringe, Donald A. "Man and Nature in Cooper's *The Praire." Nineteenth-Century Fiction,* XV (1961) 313-23.

Ross, John F. *The Social Criticism of Fenimore Cooper.* Berkeley: University of California Press, 1933.

Russell, Jason A. "Cooper: Interpreter of the Real and Historical Indian." *Journal of American History,* XXIII (1930), 41-71.

Shulenberger, Arvid. *Cooper's Theory of Fiction: His Prefaces and Their Relation to His Novels.* University of Kansas Humanities Studies, No. 32. Lawrence: University of Kansas Press, 1955.

Smith, Henry Nash. "Consciousness and Social Order: The Theme of Transcendence in the Leatherstocking Tales." *Western American Literature,* V (Fall 1970), 177-94.

Smith, Henry Nash. "Introduction." *The Prairie.* New York: Holt, Rinehart and Winston, 1950, v-xxii.

Smith, Henry Nash. *Virgin Land: The American West as Symbol and Myth.* 2nd edition. Cambridge: Harvard University Press, 1970.

Spiller, Robert E. *Fenimore Cooper: Critic of His Times.* New York: Minton, Balch, 1931.

Spiller, Robert E. *James Fenimore Cooper.* Minneapolis: University of Minnesota Press, 1965.

Spiller, Robert E. and Philip C. Blackburn. *A Descriptive Bibliography of the Writings of James Fenimore Cooper.* New York: R. R. Bowker, 1934.

Twain, Mark. "Fenimore Cooper's Literary Offenses." *North American Review*, CLXI (1895), 1-12.

Walker, Warren S. *James Fenimore Cooper: An Introduction and Interpretation.* New York: Barnes and Noble, 1962.

Walker, Warren S. "Buckskin West: Leatherstocking at High Noon." *New York Folklore Quarterly*, XXIV (June 1968), 88-102.

Waples, Dorothy. *The Whig Myth of James Fenimore Cooper.* New Haven: Yale University Press, 1938.

Wasserstrom, William. "Cooper, Freud and the Origins of Culture." *American Imago*, XVII (Winter 1960), 423-37.

Zoellner, Robert H. "Conceptual Ambivalence in Cooper's Leatherstocking." *American Literature*, XXXI (January 1960), 397-420.

GREGORY CORSO

Cook, Bruce. *The Beat Generation.* New York: Charles Scribners, 1971.

Dullea, Gerard J. "Ginsburg and Corso: Image and Imagination." *Thoth*, II (Winter 1971), 17-27.

Howard, Richard. *Alone With America: Essays in the Art of Poetry in the United States.* New York: Atheneum, 1969, 57-64.

Wilson, Robert. *A Bibliography of Works by Gregory Corso.* New York: Phoenix Book Shop, 1966.

STEPHEN CRANE

Beebe, Maurice and Thomas A. Gullason. "Criticism of Stephen Crane: A Selected Checklist with an Index to Studies of Separate Works." *Modern Fiction Studies*, V (Autumn 1959), 282-91.

Beer, Thomas. *Stephen Crane: A Study in American Letters.* New York: Knopf, 1923.

Bernard, Kenneth. " 'The Bride Comes to Yellow Sky': History as Elegy." *English Record*, XVII (April 1967), 17-20.

Berryman, John. *Stephen Crane*. New York: William Sloane, 1950.

Cady, Edwin H. *Stephen Crane*. New York: Twayne, 1962.

Cather, Willa. "When I Knew Stephen Crane." *Prairie Schooner*, XXIII (1949), 231-7.

Cook, Robert G. "Stephen Crane's 'The Bride Comes to Yellow Sky.' " *Studies in Short Fiction*, II (Summer 1965), 368-9.

Cox, James Trammell. "Stephen Crane as Symbolic Naturalist: An Analysis of 'The Blue Hotel.' " *Modern Fiction Studies*, III (Summer 1957), 147-58.

Crane, Stephen. *The Blue Hotel*, ed. Joseph Katz. Columbus, Ohio: Charles E. Merrill Publishing Company, 1969.

Garland, Hamlin. "Stephen Crane as I Knew Him." *Yale Review*, III (April 1914), 494-506.

Gibson, Donald. " 'The Blue Hotel' and the Ideal of Human Courage." *Texas Studies in Language and Literature*, VI (Autumn 1964), 388-97.

Gibson, Donald B. *The Fiction of Stephen Crane*. Carbondale, Illinois: Southern Illinois Press, 1968.

Hudspeth, Robert N., ed. "The Thoth Annual Bibliography of Stephen Crane Scholarship." *Thoth*, IV (1963), 30-58, and ff.

James, Overton Philip. "The 'Game' in 'The Bride Comes to Yellow Sky.' " *Xavier University Studies*, IV (March 1965), 3-11.

Katz, Joseph. *The Merrill Checklist of Stephen Crane*. Columbus, Ohio: Charles E. Merrill, 1969.

Katz, Joseph, ed. *Stephen Crane: The Blue Hotel*. Merrill Literary Casebook Series. Columbus, Ohio: Charles E. Merrill, 1970.

Katz, Joseph, ed. *Stephen Crane in the West and Mexico*. Kent, Ohio: Kent State University Press, 1971.

MacLean, H. N. "The Two Worlds of 'The Blue Hotel.' " *Modern Fiction Studies*, V (Autumn 1959), 260-70.

Marovitz, Sanford E. "Scratchy the Demon in 'The Bride Comes to Yellow Sky.' " *Tennessee Studies in English*, XVI (1971), 137-40.

Monteiro, George. "Stephen Crane's 'The Bride Comes to Yellow Sky.' " Neil Isaacs and Louis Leiter, eds. *Approaches to the Short Story*. San Francisco: Chandler Publishing Company, 1963, 221-38.

Paredes, Raymund A. "Stephen Crane and the Mexican." *Western American Literature*, VI (Spring 1971), 31-8.

Satterwhite, Joseph N. "Stephen Crane's 'The Blue Hotel': The Failure of Understanding." *Modern Fiction Studies*, II (Winter 1956-57), 238-41.

Slote, Bernice. "Stephen Crane in Nebraska." *Prairie Schooner*, XLIII (Summer 1969), 192-9.

Solomon, Eric. *Stephen Crane: From Parody to Realism*. Cambridge: Harvard University Press, 1967.

Stallman, R. W. *Stephen Crane: A Biography*. New York: George Braziller, 1968.

Sutton, Walter. "Pity and Fear in 'The Blue Hotel.' " *American Quarterly*, IV (Spring 1952), 73-8.

Tibbetts, A. M. "Stephen Crane's 'The Bride Comes to Yellow Sky.' " *English Journal*, LIV (April 1965), 314-6.

Van Der Beets, Richard. "Character as Structure: Ironic Parallel and Transformation in 'The Blue Hotel.' " *Studies in Short Fiction*, V (Spring 1968), 294-5.

Wertheim, Stanley. "Stephen Crane." *Hawthorne, Melville, Stephen Crane: A Critical Bibliography*, by Theodore L. Gross and Stanley Wertheim. New York: The Free Press, 1971, 203-301.

West, Ray B., Jr. "The Use of Action in 'The Bride Comes to Yellow Sky.' " *The Art of Writing Fiction*. New York: Thomas Y. Crowell Company, 1968, 134-40.

Williams, Ames W. and Vincent Starrett. *Stephen Crane: A Bibliography*. Glendale, California: John Valentine, 1948.

J. W. CRAWFORD

Nolan, Paul T. "Alaskan Men of Letters: Captain Jack Crawford." *Alaska Review*, I (Spring 1964), 41-7.

Nolan, Paul T. "J. W. Crawford: Poet-Scout of the Black Hills." *South Dakota Review*, II (Spring 1965), 40-7.

Nolan, Paul T. "Jack W. Crawford's *The Dregs*: A New Mexico Pioneer in the Short Drama." *New Mexico Quarterly*, XXXIII (1964), 388-403.

ROLLIN MALLORY DAGGETT

Weisenburger, Francis Phelps. *Idol of the West: The Fabulous Career of Rollin Mallory Daggett*. Syracuse, N.Y.: Syracuse University Press, 1965.

RICHARD HENRY DANA

Allison, James. "Journal of a Voyage from Boston to the Coast of California by Richard Henry Dana, Jr." *American Neptune*, XII (July 1952), 177-86.

Gale, Robert L. *Richard Henry Dana*. New York: Twayne, 1969.

Hart, James David. "Richard Henry Dana, Jr." Unpublished doctoral dissertation, Harvard University, 1936.

Hill, Douglas B., Jr. "Richard Henry Dana, Jr. and Two Years Before the Mast." *Criticism*, IX (Fall 1967), 312-25.

Lucid, Robert Francis. "The Composition, Reception, Reputation and Influence of Two Years Before the Mast." Unpublished doctoral dissertation, University of Chicago, 1958.

Lucid, Robert F., ed. *The Journal of Richard Henry Dana, Jr.* 3 vols. Cambridge: The Belknap Press, 1968.

H. L. DAVIS

Brunvand, Jan. "*Honey in the Horn* and 'Acres of Clams': The Regional Fiction of H. L. Davis." *Western American Literature*, II (Summer 1967), 135-45.

Bryant, Paul T. "H. L. Davis: Viable Uses for the Past." *Western American Literature*, III (Spring 1968), 3-18.

Clare, Warren L. " 'Posers, Parasites, and Pismires': *Status Rerum*, by James Stevens and H. L. Davis." *Pacific Northwest Quarterly*, LXI (January 1970), 22-30.

Etulain, Richard W. "H. L. Davis: A Bibliographical Addendum." *Western American Literature*, V (Summer 1970), 129-35.

Greiner, Francis F. "Voice of the West: Harold L. Davis." *Oregon Historical Quarterly*, LXVI (September 1965), 240-8.

Gurian, Jay. "The Unwritten West." *The American West*, II (Winter 1965), 59-63.

Hegbloom, Kirk. "H. L. Davis' Theory of Western Fiction and *Winds of Morning*." Unpublished master's thesis, University of Idaho, 1967.

Hitt, Helen. "History in Pacific Northwest Novels Written Since 1920." *Oregon Historical Quarterly*, LI (September 1950), 183-4, 195-8.

Hodgins, Francis E., Jr. "The Literary Emancipation of a Region." Unpublished doctoral dissertation, Michigan State University, 1957, 457-84.

Hutchens, John K. "H. L. Davis, Novelist: His West Lives On." *New York Times Book Review*, April 25, 1961, 23, 37.

Jenkins, Eli Seth. "H. L. Davis: A Critical Study." Unpublished doctoral dissertation, University of Southern California, 1960.

Jones, Phillip L. "The West of H. L. Davis." *South Dakota Review*, VI (Winter 1968-69), 72-84.

Kellogg, George. "H. L. Davis, 1896-1960: A Bibliography." *Texas Studies in Language and Literature*, V (Summer 1963), 294-303.

Kohler, Dayton. "H. L. Davis: Writer in the West." *College English*, XIV (December 1952), 133-40. Also in *English Journal*, XLI (December 1952), 519-26.

Lauber, John. "A Western Classic: H. L. Davis *'Honey in the Horn'.'' Western Humanities Review*, XVI (Winter 1962), 85-6.

Lorentz, Pare. "H. L. Davis: Portrait of the West." Unpublished honors thesis, Harvard College, 1959.

Mencken, H. L. "Editorial Notes." *American Mercury*, XIX (April 1930), xxvi, xxviii.

Ridgeway, Ann N., ed. *The Selected Letters of Robinson Jeffers*. Baltimore: The Johns Hopkins Press, 1968, 122-6, 177, 190.

Sanburg, Carl. "Something About H. L. Davis." *Rocky Mountain Herald*, XC (April 1, 1950), 1-2.

WILLIAM DECKER

Etulain, Richard. "Recent Western Fiction." *Journal of the West*, VIII (October 1969), 656-8.

GEORGE H. DERBY
(John Phoenix)

Delano, Alonzo. "Reminiscences of John Phoenix, Esq. the Veritable Squibob." *Hesperian*, (March 1862), 30-4.

Stewart, George R. *John Phoenix, Esq., The Veritable Squibob: A Life of Captain George H. Derby, USA*. New York: Henry Holt and Company, 1937.

Thompson, Mrs. Launt. "A Forgotten American Humorist." *The United Service Magazine*, (October 1902), 343-61.

CABEZA DE VACA

Pilkington, William T. "The Journey of Cabeza de Vaca: An American Prototype." *South Dakota Review*, VI (Spring 1968), 73-82.

BERNARD DE VOTO

Bowen, Drinker Catherine, *et. al. Four Portraits and One Subject: Bernard DeVoto*. Boston: Houghton Mifflin, 1963.

Lee, Robert Edson. *From West to East*. Urbana: University of Illinois Press, 1966, 136-52.

Lee, Robert Edson. "The Work of Bernard DeVoto, Introduction and Annotated Check List." Unpublished doctoral dissertation, State University of Iowa, 1957.

Mattingly, Garrett. *Bernard DeVoto, a Preliminary Appraisal.* Boston: Little, Brown and Company, 1938.

Pruessing, Peter Skiles. "Manifest Destiny and 'The Literary Falacy': The Paradox of Bernard DeVoto's Treatment of Westward Expansion." Unpublished master's thesis, Iowa State University, 1968.

Sawey, Orlan. *Bernard DeVoto.* New York: Twayne Publishers, Inc., 1969.

Sawey, Orlan. "Bernard DeVoto's Western Novels." *Western American Literature,* II (Fall 1967), 171-82.

Stegner, Wallace. *The Sound of Mountain Water.* New York: Doubleday and Company, Inc., 202-22.

AL DEWLEN

Merren, John. "Character and Theme in the Amarillo Novels of Al Dewlen." *Western Review,* VI (Spring 1969), 3-9.

J. FRANK DOBIE

Abernethy, Francis Edward. *J. Frank Dobie.* Southwest Writers Series, No. 1. Austin, Texas: Steck-Vaughn Company, 1967.

Bode, Winston. *A Portrait of Pancho: The Life of a Great Texan, J. Frank Dobie.* Austin, Texas: Pemberton Press, 1965.

Dobie, Bertha. "Dobie's Sunday Pieces." *Southwest Review,* L (Spring 1965), 114-9.

Dykes, Jeff. "A Dedication to the Memory of James Frank Dobie, 1888-1964." *Arizona and the West,* VIII (Autumn 1966), 203-6.

Hogue, Alexandre. "A Portrait of Pancho Dobie." *Southwest Review,* L (Spring 1965), 101-13.

McVicker, Mary Louise. *The Writings of J. Frank Dobie: A Bibliography.* Lawton, Oklahoma: Museum of the Great Plains, 1968.

Turner, Martha Anne. "Was Frank Dobie a Throwback to Mark Twain?" *Western Review,* V (Winter 1968), 3-12.

Yarborough, Ralph W. *Frank Dobie: Man and Friend.* Washington, D.C.: Potomac Corral of the Westerners, 1967.

IGNATIUS DONNELLY

Bovee, John R. "Ignatius Donnelly as a Man of Letters." Unpublished doctoral dissertation, Washington State University, 1968.

J. HYATT DOWNING

Wadden, Anthony T. "J. Hyatt Downing: The Chronicle of an Era." *Books at Iowa*, (April 1968), 11-23.
Wadden, Anthony T. "Late to the Harvest: The Fiction of J. Hyatt Downing." *Western American Literature*, VI (Fall 1971), 203-14.

GLENN WARD DRESBACH

Ford, Edsel. "Glenn Ward Dresbach: The New Mexico Years, 1915-1920." *New Mexico Quarterly*, XXXIV (1964), 78-96.

ABIGAIL SCOTT DUNIWAY

Capell, Letita Lee. "A Biography of Abigail Scott Duniway." Unpublished master's thesis, University of Oregon, 1934.
Ross, Nancy Wilson. *Westward the Woman*. New York: Alfred A. Knopf, 1945, 137-54.

JOHN C. DUVAL

Anderson, John Q. *John C. Duval: First Texas Man of Letters.* Southwest Writers Series, No. 2. Austin, Texas: Steck-Vaughn Company, 1967.
Dobie, J. Frank. *John C. Duval, First Texas Man of Letters: His Life and Some of His Unpublished Writings.* Dallas: Southern Methodist University Press, 1939.

EVA EMERY DYE

Ellingsen, Melva G. "Eva and Clio; or, the Muse Meets Its Mistress." *The Call Number*, XIX (Fall 1957), 17-22.
Powers, Alfred. *History of Oregon Literature.* Portland: Metropolitan Press, 1935, 404-14.

Taber, Ronald W. "Sacagawea and the Suffragettes." *Pacific Northwest Quarterly*, LVIII (January 1967), 7-13.

WILLIAM EASTLAKE

Angell, Richard C. "Eastlake: At Home and Abroad." *New Mexico Quarterly*, XXXIV (Summer 1964), 204-9.

Haslam, Gerald. *William Eastlake*. Southwest Writers Series, No. 36. Austin, Texas: Steck-Vaughn Company, 1970.

Haslam, Gerry. "William Eastlake: Portrait of the Artist as Shaman." *Western Review*, VIII (Spring 1971), 2-13.

Milton, John R. "The Land as Form in Frank Waters and William Eastlake." *Kansas Quarterly*, II (Spring 1970), 104-9.

Woolf, Douglas. "One of the Truly Good Men." *Evergreen Review*, II (Spring 1959), 194-6.

Wylder, Delbert E. "The Novels of William Eastlake." *New Mexico Quarterly*, XXXIV (Summer 1964), 188-203.

EDWARD EGGLESTON

Johannsen, Robert W. "Literature and History: The Early Novels of Edward Eggleston." *Indiana Magazine of History*, XLVIII (March 1952), 37-54.

Randel, William Pierce. *Edward Eggleston*. Gloucester, Massachusetts: Peter Smith, 1962.

Randel, William Pierce. "Edward Eggleston (1837-1902)." *American Literary Realism*, I (Fall 1967), 36-8.

Randel, William Pierce. "Edward Eggleston's Minnesota Fiction." *Minnesota History*, XXXIII (Spring 1953), 189-93.

LOULA GRACE ERDMAN

Sewell, Ernestine. *Loula Grace Erdman*. Southwest Writers Series, No. 33. Austin, Texas: Steck-Vaughn Company, 1970.

HELEN EUSTIS

Burns, Stuart L. "St. Petersburg Re-Visited: Helen Eustis and Mark Twain." *Western American Literature*, V (Summer 1970), 99-112.

MAX EVANS

Milton, John R., ed. "Interview: Max Evans." *South Dakota Review,* V (Summer 1967), 77-87.

Milton, John R. *Three West: Conversations with Vardis Fisher, Max Evans, Michael Straight.* Vermillion, South Dakota: Dakota Press, 1970.

Sonnichsen, C. L. "The New Style Western." *South Dakota Review,* IV (Summer 1966), 22-8.

WILLIAM EVERSON
(Brother Antoninus)

Cargas, H. J. "An Interview with Brother Antoninus." *Renascence,* XVIII (Spring 1966), 137-45.

McDonnell, T. P. "Poet from the West: Evenings with Brother Antoninus." *Commonweal,* LXXVIII (March 29, 1963), 13-4.

Rizzo, Fred F. "A Study of the Poetry of William Everson." Unpublished doctoral dissertation, University of Oklahoma, 1966.

Stafford, William E., ed. *The Achievement of Brother Antoninus: A Comprehensive Selection of His Poems With a Critical Introduction.* Glenview, Illinois: Scott, Foresman, 1967.

FREDERICK FAUST
See Luke Short

FREDERICK FEIKEMA
See Frederick Feikema Manfred

EDNA FERBER

Brenni, V. J., and B. L. Spencer. "Edna Ferber: A Selected Bibliography." *Bulletin of Bibliography,* XXII (September-December 1958), 152-6.

Overton, Grant. "Edna Ferber." *The Women Who Make Our Novels.* New York: Dodd Mead, 1928, 126-38.

ERNA FERGUSSON

Remley, David A. *Erna Fergusson.* Southwest Writers Series, No. 24. Austin, Texas: Steck-Vaughn Company, 1969.

HARVEY FERGUSSON

Baldwin, Charles C. "Harvey Fergusson." *The Men Who Make Our Novels*. New York: Dodd, Mead and Company, 1924, 154-65.

Fergusson, Erna. *New Mexico: A Pageant of Three Peoples*. New York, 1952.

Folsom, James K. *Harvey Fergusson*. Southwest Writers Series, No. 20. Austin, Texas: Steck-Vaughn Company, 1969.

McGinity, Sue Simmons. "Harvey Fergusson's Use of Animal Imagery in Characterizing Spanish-American Women." *Western Review*, VIII (Winter 1971), 46-50.

Milton, John. "Conversation with Harvey Fergusson." *South Dakota Review*, IX (Spring 1971), 39-45.

Pearson, Lorene. "Harvey Fergusson and the Crossroads." *New Mexico Quarterly*, XXI (Autumn 1951), 334-55.

Pilkington, William T. "The Southwestern Novels of Harvey Fergusson." *New Mexico Quarterly*, XXXV (Winter 1965-66), 330-43.

Robinson, Cecil. *With the Ears of Strangers: The Mexican in American Literature*. Tucson: University of Arizona Press, 1963.

Thrift, Bonnie, B. R. "Harvey Fergusson's Use of Southwest History and Customs in His Novels." Unpublished master's thesis, University of Texas, 1940.

LAWRENCE FERLINGHETTI

Butler, J. A. "Ferlinghetti: Dirty Old Man?" *Renascence*, XVIII (Spring 1966), 115-23.

Cook, Bruce. *The Beat Generation*. New York: Charles Scribners, 1971.

Ianni, L. A. "Lawrence Ferlinghetti's Fourth Person Singular and the Theory of Relativity." *Wisconsin Studies in Contemporary Literature*, VIII (Summer 1967), 392-406.

THOMAS HORNSBY FERRIL

Effinger, Cecil. "Music in the Poems of Thomas Hornsby Ferril." *Colorado Quarterly*, III (Summer 1954), 59-66.

Richards, Robert F. "The Long Dimension of Ferril's Poetry." *Colorado Quarterly*, III (Summer 1954), 22-38.

Richards, Robert F. "The Poetry of Thomas Hornsby Ferril." Unpublished doctoral dissertation, Columbia University, 1961.

Richards, Robert F. "Thomas Hornsby Ferril and the Problems of the Poet in the West." *Kansas Quarterly*, II (Spring 1970), 110-6.

LESLIE FIEDLER

Bellman, S. I. "The American Artist as European Frontiersman: Leslie Fiedler's *The Second Stone.*" *Critique*, VI (1963), 131-43.
Bellman, S. I. "The Frontiers of Leslie Fiedler." *Southwest Review*, XLVIII (1963), 86-9.
Feinstein, Herbert. "Contemporary American Fiction: Harvey Swados and Leslie Fiedler." *Wisconsin Studies in Contemporary Literature*, II (Winter 1961), 79-98.
Schultz, Max F. *Radical Sophistication: Studies in Contemporary Jewish-American Novelists.* Athens: Ohio University Press, 1969, 154-72.

VARDIS FISHER

American Book Collector. XIV (September 1963), 7-39. Special Fisher Number.
Bishop, John Peale. "The Strange Case of Vardis Fisher." *The Collected Essays of John Peale Bishop.* New York: Charles Scribner's Sons, 1948, 56-65.
Bishop, John Peale. "The Strange Case of Vardis Fisher." *The Southern Review*, III (Autumn 1937), 348-59.
Day, George Frederic. "The Uses of History in the Novels of Vardis Fisher." Unpublished doctoral dissertation, University of Colorado, 1968.
Fisher, Vardis. "The Western Writer and the Eastern Establishment." *Western American Literature*, I (Winter 1967), 244-59.
Flora, Joseph M. *Vardis Fisher.* New York: Twayne Publishers, 1965.
Flora, Joseph M. "Vardis Fisher and the Mormons." *Dialogue: A Journal of Mormon Thought*, IV (Autumn 1969), 48-55.
Flora, Joseph M. "Vardis Fisher and James Branch Cabell: An Essay on Influence and Reputation." *The Cabellian*, II (Autumn 1969), 12-6.
Flora, Joseph M. "Vardis Fisher and Wallace Stegner: Teacher and Student." *Western American Literature*, V (Summer 1970), 121-8.
Grover, Dorys N. "A Study of the Poetry of Vardis Fisher." Unpublished doctoral dissertation, Washington State University, 1970.

Hanks, Ida Mae. "Antelope, Idaho, in the Novels of Vardis Fisher." Unpublished master's thesis, University of Idaho, 1942.

Kellogg, George. "Vardis Fisher: A Bibliography." *Western American Literature*, V (Spring 1970), 45-64.

Long, Louise. "Children of God." *Southwest Review*, XXV (October 1939), 102-8.

Milton, John R. *Three West: Conversations with Vardis Fisher, Max Evans, Michael Straight.* Vermillion, South Dakota: Dakota Press, 1970.

Milton, John. "Vardis Fisher: March 31, 1895-July 9, 1968." *Western American Literature*, III (Summer 1968), 114.

Rein, David. *Vardis Fisher: Challenge to Evasion.* Chicago: Black Cat Press, Normandie House, 1937.

Snell, George. *Shapers of American Fiction.* New York: E. P. Dutton & Co. Inc., 1943, 276-88.

Taber, Ronald. "Vardis Fisher and the *Idaho Guide:* Preserving Culture for the New Deal." *Pacific Northwest Quarterly*, LIX (April 1968), 68-76.

Taber, Ronald. "Vardis Fisher: March 31, 1895-July 9, 1968." *Idaho Yesterdays*, XII (Fall 1968), 2-8.

Taber, Ronald W. "Vardis Fisher: New Directions for the Historical Novel." *Western American Literature*, I (Winter 1967), 285-96.

Thomas, Alfred Krupp. "The Epic of Evolution, Its Etiology and Art: A Study of Vardis Fisher's *Testament of Man.*" Unpublished doctoral dissertation, Pennsylvania State University, 1967.

TIMOTHY FLINT

Flint, Timothy. *Recollections of the Last Ten Years.* Boston, 1826; New York: Alfred A. Knopf, 1932.

Folsom, James K. *Timothy Flint.* New York: Twayne Publishers, 1965.

Hamilton, John A. "Timothy Flint's 'Lost Novel.' " *American Literature*, XXII (March 1950), 54-6.

Kirkpatrick, John Ervin. *Timothy Flint.* Cleveland: Arthur H. Clark, 1911.

Lee, Robert Edson. *From West to East.* Urbana: University of Illinois Press, 1966, 39-54.

Lombard, C. "Timothy Flint: Early American Disciple of French Romanticism." *Revue de Littérature Comparée*, XXXVI (Avril-Juin 1962), 276-82.

Morris, Robert L. "Three Arkansas Travelers." *Arkansas Historical Quarterly*, IV (Autumn 1945), 215-30.

Seelye, John D. "Timothy Flint's 'Wicked River' and *The Confidence Man*." *PMLA*, LXXVIII (March 1963), 75-9.

Stimson, Frederick S. " 'Francis Berrian': Hispanic Influence on American Romanticism." *Hispanica*, XLII (December 1959), 511-6.

Turner, Arlin. "James K. Paulding and Timothy Flint." *Mississippi Valley Historical Review*, XXXIV (June 1947), 105-11.

Vorpahl, Ben Merchant. "The Eden Theme and Three Novels by Timothy Flint." *Studies in Romanticism*, X (Spring 1971), 105-29.

Walker, Lennie Merle. "Picturesque New Mexico Revealed in Novels as Early as 1826." *New Mexico Quarterly Review*, XIII (July 1938), 325-8.

ROBERT FLYNN

Etulain, Richard. "Recent Western Fiction." *Journal of the West*, VIII (October 1969), 656-8.

MARY HALLOCK FOOTE

Benn, Mary Lou. "Mary Hallock Foote: Early Leadville Writer." *Colorado Magazine*, XXXIII (April 1956), 93-108.

Benn, Mary Lou. "Mary Hallock Foote in Idaho." *University of Wyoming Publications*, XX (July 1956), 157-78.

Benn, Mary Lou. "Mary Hallock Foote: Pioneer Woman Novelist." Unpublished master's thesis, University of Wyoming, 1955.

Foote, Arthur B. "Memoir of Arthur De Wint Foot." *Transactions of the American Society of Civil Engineers*, XCIX (1934), 1449-52.

Taft, Robert. *Artists and Illustrators of the Old West: 1850-1900*. New York: Charles Scribner's Sons, 1953, 172-5, 345-7.

WAYNE GARD

Adams, Ramon F. *Wayne Gard: Historian of the West*. Southwest Writers Series, No. 31. Austin, Texas: Steck-Vaughn Company, 1970.

HAMLIN GARLAND

Ahnebrink, Lars. *The Beginnings of Naturalism in American Fiction.* Upsala, 1950, 63-89.

Alsen, Eberhard. "Hamlin Garland's First Novel: *A Spoil of Office.*" *Western American Literature,* IV (Summer 1969), 91-105.

Arvidson, Lloyd A., ed. *Centennial Tributes and a Checklist of the Hamlin Garland Papers in the University of Southern California Library.* Los Angeles: University of Southern California Library, 1962.

Bryer, Jackson R., and Eugene Harding. "Hamlin Garland (1860-1940): A Bibliography of Secondary Comment." *American Literary Realism 1870-1910,* III (Fall 1970), 290-387.

Bryer, Jackson R., and Eugene Harding. "Hamlin Garland: Reviews and Notices of His Work." *American Literary Realism 1870-1910,* IV (Spring 1971), 102-56.

Duffey, Bernard. "Hamlin Garland's 'Decline' from Realism." *American Literature,* XXV (March 1953), 69-74.

French, Warren. "What Shall We Do About Hamlin Garland?" *American Literary Realism 1870-1910, III (Fall 1970), 283-9.*

Fujii, Gertrude Sugioka. "The Veritism of Hamlin Garland." Unpublished doctoral dissertation, University of Southern California, 1970.

Garland, Hamlin. "The West in Literature." *Arena,* VI (1892), 669-76.

Harris, Elbert L. "Hamlin Garland's Use of the American Scene in His Fiction." Unpublished doctoral dissertation, University of Pennsylvania, 1959.

Harrison, Stanley R. "Hamlin Garland and the Double Vision of Naturalism." *Studies in Short Fiction,* VI (Fall 1969), 548-56.

Holloway, Jean. *Hamlin Garland: A Biography.* Austin: University of Texas Press, 1960.

Holsinger, Paul M. "Hamlin Garland's Colorado." *The Colorado Magazine,* XLIV (Winter 1967), 1-10.

Houston, Neal B. "A Dedication to . . . Hamlin Garland: 1860-1940." *Arizona and the West,* XI (Autumn 1969), 209-12.

Mane, Robert. *Hamlin Garland: L'Homme et L'oeuvre (1860-1940).* Paris: Didier, 1968.

Higgins, J. E. "A Man from the Middle Borders: Hamlin Garland's Diaries." *Wisconsin Magazine of History,* XLVI (Summer 1963), 295-302.

Meyer, Roy W. "Hamlin Garland and the American Indian." *Western American Literature,* II (Summer 1967), 109-25.

Miller, Charles T. "Hamlin Garland's Retreat from Realism." *Western American Literature,* I (Summer 1966), 119-29.

Morgan, H. Wayne. *American Writers in Rebellion: From Mark Twain to Dreiser.* New York: Hill and Wang, 1965.

Neumann, Edwin J. "Hamlin Garland and the Mountain West." Unpublished doctoral dissertation, Northwestern University, 1951.

Pizer, Donald. "Hamlin Garland (1860-1938)." *American Literary Realism 1870-1910,* I (Fall 1967), 45-51.

Pizer, Donald. "Hamlin Garland: A Bibliography of Newspaper and Periodical Publications. (1885-1895)." *Bulletin of Bibliography,* XXII (January-April 1957), 41-4.

Pizer, Donald. "Hamlin Garland's *A Son of the Middle Border:* An Appreciation." *South Atlantic Quarterly,* LXV (Autumn 1966), 448-59.

Pizer, Donald. "Hamlin Garland's *A Son of the Middle Border: Autobiography as Art."* in *Essays in American and English Literature Presented to Bruce Robert McElderry, Jr.,* edited Max F. Schultz, *et. al.* Athens: Ohio University Press, 1967.

Pizer, Donald, ed. *Hamlin Garland's Diaries.* San Marino, California: Huntington Library, 1968.

Pizer, Donald. *Hamlin Garland's Early Works and Career.* Berkeley: University of California Press, 1960.

Reamer, Owen J. "Garland and the Indians." *New Mexico Quarterly,* XXXIV (Autumn 1964), 257-80.

Reamer, Owen J. "Hamlin Garland: Literary Pioneer and Typical American." Unpublished doctoral dissertation, University of Texas, 1951.

Simpson, Claude M., Jr. "Hamlin Garland's Decline." *Southwest Review,* XXVI (1941), 223-34.

Walcutt, Charles Child. *American Literary Naturalism, A Divided Stream.* Minneapolis: University of Minnesota Press, 1956, 53-65 and *passim.*

Whitford, Kathryn. "Crusader Without a Cause: An Examination of Hamlin Garland's Middle Border." *Midcontinent American Studies Journal,* VI (Spring 1965), 61-72.

Whitford, Kathryn. "Patterns of Observation: A Study of Hamlin Garland's Middle Border Landscape." *Transactions of the Wisconsin Academy of Science, Arts, and Letters,* L (1961), 331-8.

HECTOR LEWIS GARRARD
(Lewis H. Garrad)

Bewley, Marius. *"Wah-To-Yah and the Taos Trail:* A Minor Classic." *Masks and Mirrors.* New York: Atheneum, 1970, 221-5.

Guthrie, A. B., Jr. "Introduction." *Wah-To-Yah and the Taos Trail.*
Norman: University of Oklahoma Press, 1955, ix-xvi.

FRIEDRICH GERSTÄCKER

Kolb, Alfred. "Friedrich Gerstäcker and the American Frontier."
Unpublished doctoral dissertation, Syracuse University, 1966.
Kolb, Alfred. "Gërstacker's America." *Thoth*, VII (Winter 1966), 12-21.
Steeves, Harrison R. "The First of the Westerns." *Southwest Review*,
LIII (Winter 1968), 74-84.

ALLEN GINSBERG

Bett, Carolyn E. "The Poetry of Allen Ginsberg." Unpublished
master's thesis, University of Toronto, 1967.
Cook, Bruce. *The Beat Generation.* New York: Charles Scribners,
1971.
Eckman, Frederick. "Neither Tame nor Fleecy." *Poetry*, XC (September 1957), 386-97.
Ehrlich, J. W. *Howl of the Censor.* San Carlos, California, 1961.
Golffing, Francis, and Barbara Gibbs. "The Public Voice: Remarks
on Poetry Today." *Commentary*, XXVIII (July 1959), 63-9.
Kramer, Jane. *Allen Ginsberg in America.* New York: Random
House, 1968.
Menkin, E. Z. "Allen Ginsberg: A Bibliographical and Biographical
Sketch." *Thoth*, VIII (Winter 1967), 35-40.
Merrill, Thomas F. *Allen Ginsberg.* New York: Twayne Publishers,
1969.
Rosenthal, M. L. *The New Poetry.* New York: Macmillan, 1967.
Ruamker, Michael. "Allen Ginsberg's *Howl.* " *Black Mountain
Review*, VII (Autumn 1957), 228-37.
Trilling, Diana. "The Other Night at Columbia." *Partisan Review*,
XXVI (Spring 1959), 214-30.

FRED GIPSON

Henderson, Sam H. *Fred Gipson.* Southwest Writers Series, No. 10.
Austin, Texas: Steck Vaughn Company, 1967.

FREDERICK GLIDDEN
See Luke Short

ZANE GREY

Bauer, Erwin A. "Ohio's Writer of the Purple Sage," in Zane Grey, *Blue Feather and Other Stories*. New York: Harper and Brothers, 1961, 229-34.

Etulain, Richard W. "A Dedication to . . . Zane Grey 1872-1939." *Arizona and the West*, XII (Autumn 1970), 217-20.

Gentles, Ruth G. *The Zane Grey Omnibus*. New York: Harper and Brothers, 1943.

Grey, Zane. "Breaking Through: The Story of My Life." *American Magazine*, (July 1924), 11-3 ff.

Gruber, Frank. *Zane Grey: A Biography*. New York: The World Publishing Company, 1970.

Karr, Jean. *Zane Grey: Man of the West*. New York: Greenberg Publishers, 1949.

Patrick, A. "Getting into Six Figures: Zane Grey." *Bookman*, LX (December 1924), 424-9.

Powell, L. C. "Books Determine." *Wilson Library Bulletin*, XXX (September 1955), 62-5.

Rascoe, Burton. "Opie Read and Zane Grey." *Saturday Review of Literature*, XXI (November 11, 1939), 8.

Whipple, T. K. "American Sagas." *Study Out the Land*. Berkeley: University of California Press, 1943, 19-29.

JOHN HOWARD GRIFFIN

Campbell, Jeff H. *John Howard Griffin*. Southwest Writers Series, No. 35. Austin, Texas: Steck-Vaughn Company, 1970.

Geismar, Maxwell. "John Howard Griffin: The Devil in Texas." *American Moderns*. New York: Hill and Wang, 1958, 251-65.

McDonnell, Thomas P. "John Howard Griffin: An Interview." *Ramparts*, I (January 1963), 6-16.

A. B. GUTHRIE

Breit, Harvey. "Talk with A. B. Guthrie, Jr." *New York Times Book Review*. October 23, 1949, 39.

Cracroft, Richard H. *"The Big Sky:* A. B. Guthrie's Use of Historical Sources." *Western American Literature*, VI (Fall 1971), 163-76.

Etulain, Richard W. "A. B. Guthrie: A Bibliography." *Western American Literature*, IV (Summer 1969), 133-8.

Falk, Armand. "The Riddle of Experience." Unpublished master's thesis, University of Montana, 1965.

Folsom, James K. *The American Western Novel.* New Haven: *College and University Press, 1966, 64-76.*

Ford, Thomas W. *A. B. Guthrie, Jr.* Southwest Writers Series, No. 15. Austin, Texas: Steck-Vaughn Company, 1968.

Guthrie, A. B., Jr. *The Blue Hen's Chick.* New York: McGraw-Hill Book Company, 1965.

Hodgins, Francis E., Jr. "The Literary Emancipation of a Region . . ." Unpublished doctoral dissertation, Michigan State University, 1957, 485-517.

Kite, Merilyn. "A. B. Guthrie, Jr.: A Critical Evaluation of His Works." Unpublished master's thesis, University of Wyoming, 1965.

Kohler, Dayton. "A. B. Guthrie, Jr. and the West." *College English*, XII (February 1951), 249-56. Also in *English Journal*, XI, (February 1951), 65-72.

Mitchell, Mildred. "The Women in A. B. Guthrie's Novels." Unpublished master's thesis, Southwest Texas State College, 1965.

Putnam, Jackson K. "Down to Earth: A. B. Guthrie's Quest for Moral and Historical Truth." *Essays on Western History . . .* Grand Forks: University of North Dakota Press, 51-61.

Stegner, Wallace. "Foreword." Sentry Edition of *The Big Sky.* Boston: Houghton Mifflin Company, 1965.

Stephan, Peter M. "Fact, Interpretation, and Theme in the Historical Novels of A. B. Guthrie, Jr." Unpublished master's thesis, North Texas State University, 1968.

Stineback, David C. "On History and Its Consequences: A. B. Guthrie's *These Thousand Hills.*" *Western American Literature*, VI (Fall 1971), 177-89.

Walker, Don D. "The Mountain Man as Literary Hero." *Western American Literature*, I (Spring 1966), 15-25.

Williams, John. "The 'Western': Definition of the Myth." *Nation*, CXCIII (November 18, 1961), 401-6.

Young, Vernon. "An American Dream and Its Parody." *Arizona Quarterly*, VI (Summer 1950), 112-23.

JOHN HAINES

Allen, Carolyn J. "Death and Dreams in John Haine's *Writer's News.*" *Alaska Review*, III (Fall-Winter 1969), 28-36.

Wilson, James R. "Relentless Self-Scrutiny: The Poetry of John Haines." *Alaska Review*, III (Fall-Winter 1969), 16-27.

DICK WICK HALL

Boyer, Mary G., ed. "Dick Wick Hall." *Arizona in Literature.* Glendale, California: The Arthur H. Clarke Co., 1935, 495-511.

Mitten, Irma Catherine. "The Life and Literary Career of Dick Wick Hall, Arizona Humorist." Unpublished master's thesis, University of Southern California, 1940.

Myers, Samuel L. "Dick Wick Hall: Humorist with a Serious Purpose." *Journal of Arizona History,* XI (Winter 1970), 255-78.

Nutt, Francis Dorothy. *Dick Wick Hall: Stories From the Salome Sun by Arizona's Most Famous Humorist.* Flagstaff: Northland Press, 1968.

HAZEL HALL

Powell, L. C. "A Note on Hazel Hall and Her Poetry." *General Magazine and Historical Chronicle,* XXXVII (1933), 14-25.

JAMES HALL

Donald, David. "The Autobiography of James Hall, Western Literary Pioneer." *Ohio State Archaeological and Historical Quarterly,* LVI (1947), 295-304.

Flanagan, John T. *James Hall, Literary Pioneer of the Ohio Valley.* Minneapolis: University of Minnesota Press, 1941.

Lee, Robert Edson. *From West to East.* Urbana: University of Illinois Press, 1966, 54-7.

Randall, Randolph C. *James Hall, Spokesman of the New West.* Columbus: Ohio State University Press, 1964.

Todd, Edgeley W. "The Authorship of 'The Missouri Trapper.' " *Missouri Historical Society Bulletin,* XV (1959), 194-200.

Todd, Edgeley W. "James Hall and the Hugh Glass Legend." *American Quarterly,* VII (1955), 362-70.

BRET HARTE

Boggan, J. R. "The Regeneration of 'Roaring Camp.' " *Nineteenth-Century Fiction,* XXII (December 1967), 271-80.

Booth, Bradford. "Unpublished Letters of Bret Harte." *American Literature,* XVI (May 1944), 131-42.

Boynton, Henry W. *Bret Harte*. New York: McLure, Phillips, and Company, 1903.

Brady, Duer S. "A New Look at Bret Harte and the *Overland Monthly.*" Unpublished doctoral dissertation, University of Arkansas, 1962.

Brown, Allen B. "The Christ Motif in 'The Luck of Roaring Camp.' " *Papers of the Michigan Academy of Sciences, Art, and Letters,* XLVI (1961), 629-33.

Duckett, Margaret. "Bret Harte and the Indians of Northern California." *Huntington Library Quarterly,* XVIII (November 1954), 59-83.

Duckett, Margaret. "Bret Harte's Portrayal of Half-Breeds." *American Literature,* XXV (May 1953), 193-212.

Duckett, Margaret. *Mark Twain and Bret Harte*. Norman: University of Oklahoma Press, 1964.

Duckett, Margaret. "Plain Language from Bret Harte." *Nineteenth Century Fiction,* XI (March 1957), 241-60.

Erskine, John. "Bret Harte." *Leading American Novelists.* New York, 1910, 325-69.

Gaer, Joseph, ed. *Bret Harte: Bibliography and Biographical Data.* New York: Burt Franklin, 1968.

Harrison, Joseph B., ed. *Bret Harte: Representative Selections.* New York: American Book Company, 1941.

Harte, Bret. *The Letters of Bret Harte,* ed. Geoffrey Bret Harte. Boston: Houghton Mifflin Company, 1926.

Hazard, Lucy L. "Eden to Eldorado." *University of California Chronicle,* XXXV (January 1933), 107-21.

May, Ernest. "Bret Harte and the *Overland Monthly.*" *American Literature,* XXII (1950), 260-71.

May, Ernest R. "The *Overland Monthly* under Bret Harte." Unpublished master's thesis, University of California at Los Angeles, 1949.

Merwin, Henry C. "Bret Harte's Heroines." *Atlantic Monthly,* CII (September 1908), 297-307.

Merwin, Henry Childs. *The Life of Bret Harte.* Boston: Houghton Mifflin Company, 1911.

Morrow, Patrick. "Bret Harte (1836-1902)." *American Literary Realism 1870-1910,* III (Spring 1970), 167-77.

Morrow, Patrick. "The Literary Criticism of Bret Harte." Unpublished doctoral dissertation, University of Washington, 1969.

O'Brien, Dominic Vincent. "Bret Harte: A Survey of the Criticism of His Work." Unpublished doctoral dissertation, University of Pennsylvania, 1968.

O'Connor, Richard. *Bret Harte: A Biography.* Boston: Little, Brown & Co., 1966.

Oliver, E. S. "The Pig-tailed China Boys out West." *Western Humanities Review*, XII (Spring 1958), 159-78.

Overland Monthly [Special Bret Harte Number], XL (September 1902).

Pattee, Fred Lewis. "Bret Harte." *The Development of the American Short Story*. New York: 1923, 220-44.

Pattee, Fred Lewis. "Bret Harte." *A History of American Literature Since 1870.* New York, 1922, 63-82.

Stegner, Wallace. "The West Synthetic: Bret Harte." *The Sound of Mountain Water*. Garden City: Doubleday and Company, 1969, 23-36.

Stewart, George R., Jr. *Bret Harte: Argonaut and Exile*. Boston: Houghton Mifflin Company, 1931.

Stewart, George R. "The Bret Harte Legend." *University of California Chronicle*, XXX (July 1928), 338-50.

Stewart, George R. "Bret Harte on the Frontier." *Southwest Review*, XI (April 1926), 265-73.

Timpe, Eugene F. "Bret Harte's German Public." *Jahrbuch fur Amerikastudien*, X (1965), 215-20.

WALTER HAVIGHURST

Jones, Joel M. "To Feel the Heartland's Pulse: The Writing of Walter Havighurst." *Kansas Quarterly*, II (Spring 1970), 88-96.

ERNEST HAYCOX

DeVoto, Bernard. "Phaëton on Gunsmoke Trail." *Harpers*, CCIX (December 1954), 10-11 ff.

"Ernest Haycox Memorial Number." *Call Number*, XXV (1963-64), 1-31.

Etulain, Richard W. "Ernest Haycox: The Historical Western, 1937-43," *South Dakota Review*, V (Spring 1967), 35-54.

Etulain, Richard W. "The Literary Career of a Western Writer: Ernest Haycox 1899-1950." Unpublished doctoral dissertation, University of Oregon, 1966.

Fargo, James. "The Western and Ernest Haycox," *The Prairie Schooner*, XXVI (Summer 1952), 177-84.

ALICE CORBIN HENDERSON

Pearce, T. M. *Alice Corbin Henderson*. Southwest Writers Series, No. 21. Austin, Texas: Steck-Vaughn Company, 1969.

O. HENRY
See William Sydney Porter

WILL HENRY
(Henry Wilson Allen)

Needham, Arnold E. "[An Essay Review of three Will Henry Books]." *Western American Literature*, I (Winter 1967), 297-302.

ELLA HIGGINSON

Reynolds, Helen Louise. "Ella Higginson: Northwest Author." Unpublished master's thesis, University of Washington, 1941.
Vore, Elizabeth. "Ella Higginson, A Successful Pacific Coast Writer." *Overland*, XXXIII (May 1899), 434-6.

EDWIN B. HILL

Myers, John Myers. "A Checklist of Items Published by the Private Press of Edwin B. Hill." *American Book Collector*, XVIII (October 1967), 22-7.

PAUL HORGAN

Carter, Alfred. "On the Fiction of Paul Horgan." *New Mexico Quarterly*, VII (August 1937), 207-16.
Day, James M. *Paul Horgan*. Southwest Writers Series, No. 8. Austin, Texas: Steck-Vaughn Company, 1967.
Lindenau, Judith W. "Paul Horgan's *Mountain Standard Time.*" *South Dakota Review*, I(May 1964), 57-64.
McConnell, Richard M. M., and Susan A. Frey. "Paul Horgan: A Bibliography." *Western American Literature*, VI (Summer 1971), 137-50.
McConnell, Richard M. M., and Susan A. Frey. *Paul Horgan's Humble Powers: A Bibliography*. Washington, D. C.: Information Resources Press, 1971.
Reeve, Frank Durer. "A Letter to Clio." *New Mexico Historical Review*, XXXI (April 1956), 102-32.

EMERSON HOUGH

Gaston, Edwin W., Jr. *The Early Novel of the Southwest.*
Albuquerque: University of New Mexico Press, 1961.

Grahame, Pauline. "A Novelist of the Unsung." *The Palimpsest,* XI
(1930), 67-77.

Henry, Stuart. *Conquering Our Great American Plains: A Historical
Development.* New York, 1930.

Hutchinson, W. H. *A Bar Cross Man: The Life and Writings of
Eugene Manlove Rhodes. Norman: University of Oklahoma
Press, 1956.*

Hutchinson, W. H. "Grassfire on the Great Plains." *Southwest
Review,* XLI (Spring 1956), 181-5.

Stone, Lee Alexander. *Emerson Hough: His Place in American
Letters.* Chicago, 1925.

Wylder, Delbert E. *Emerson Hough.* Southwest Writers Series, No.
19. Austin, Texas: Steck-Vaughn Company, 1969.

Wylder, D. E. "Emerson Hough's *Heart's Desires:* Revisit to Eden."
Western American Literature, I (Spring 1966), 44-54.

EDGAR WATSON HOWE

Brune, Ruth E. "The Early Life of Edgar Watson Howe." Unpublished doctoral dissertation, University of Colorado, 1949.

Brune, Ruth E. "Ed Howe in the *Golden Globe.*" *Western
Humanities Review,* VIII (Autumn 1954), 365-8.

Dick, Everett. "Ed Howe, a Notable Figure on the Sod-House
Frontier." *Nebraska History Magazine,* XVIII (April-June
1937), 138-43.

Howe, E. W. *Plain People.* New York: Dodd, Mead and Company,
1929.

Pickett, Calder M. *Ed Howe: Country Town Philosopher.* Lawrence:
The University Press of Kansas, 1968.

Pickett, Calder M. "Edgar Watson Howe and the Kansas Scene."
Kansas Quarterly, II (Spring 1970), 39-45.

Pickett, Calder M. "Edgar Watson Howe: Legend and Truth."
American Literary Realism 1870-1910, II (Spring 1969), 70-3.

Powers, Richard. "Tradition in E. W. Howe's *The Story of a Country
Town.*" *Midcontinent American Studies Journal,* IX (Fall 1968),
51-62.

Ropp, Philip H. "Edgar Watson Howe." Unpublished doctoral
dissertation, University of Virginia, 1949.

Schorer, C. E. "Growing Up with the Country." *Midwest Journal,* VI
(Fall 1954) 12-26.

Simpson, Claude, M. "Introduction." in *Story of a Country Town*. Cambridge: Harvard University Press, 1961, vii-xxxi.

Stronks, James B. "William Dean Howells, Ed Howe, and *The Story of a Country Town*." *American Literature*, XXIX (January 1958), 473-8.

Ward, John William. "Afterword." in E. W. Howe, *The Story of a Country Town*. New York: Signet, 1964, 299-309.

Woodhouse, William Lloyd. "The Writings and Philosophy of E. W. Howe." Unpublished master's thesis, University of Kansas, 1941.

WILLIAM HUMPHREY

Boatright, James. "William Humphrey (1924-   )." *A Bibliographical Guide to the Study of Southern Literature*, ed. Louis D. Rubin, Jr. Baton Rouge: Louisiana State University Press, 1969, 224-5.

Hoffman, Frederick J. *The Art of Southern Fiction*. Carbondale: Illinois University Press, 1967, 103-6.

Lee, James W. *William Humphrey*. Southwest Writers Series, No. 7. Austin: Steck-Vaughn Company, 1967.

Rubin, Louis D., Jr. *The Curious Death of the Novel*. Baton Rouge: Louisiana State University Press, 1967, 263-5 ff.

LUIS INCLÁN

Paredes, Americo. "Luis Inclán: First of the Cowboy Writers." *American Quarterly*, XII (Spring 1960), 55-70.

WILLIAM INGE

Barrett, Charles M. "William Inge: The Mid-Century Playwright." Unpublished master's thesis, University of North Carolina at Chapel Hill, 1957.

Herron, Ima Honaker. "Our Vanishing Towns: Modern Broadway Versions" *Southwest Review*, LI (1966), 209-20.

Manley, Francis. "William Inge: A Bibliography." *American Book Collector*, XVI (1965), 13-21.

Miller, Jordan Y. "William Inge: Last of the Realists?" *Kansas Quarterly*, II (Spring 1970), 17-26.

Shuman, R. Baird. *William Inge*. New York: Twayne Publishers, 1965.

Weales, Gerald. *American Drama Since World War II*. New York: Harcourt, Brace and World, 1962.

WASHINGTON IRVING

Beach, Leonard B. "American Literature Re-Examined: Washington Irving, the Artist in a Changing World." *University of Kansas City Review*, XIV (1948), 259-66.

Gardner, J. H. "One Hundred Years Ago in the Region of Tulsa." *Chronicles of Oklahoma*, XI (June 1933), 765-85.

Hudson, Ruth. "A Literary 'Area of Freedom' Between Irving and Twain." *Western Humanities Review*, XIII (Winter 1959), 46-60.

Irving, Pierre M. *The Life and Letters of Washington Irving.* 4 vols. New York: Putnam, 1862-1864.

Irving, Washington. *A Tour of the Prairies*, edited with introduction by John Francis McDermott. Norman: University of Oklahoma Press, 1956.

Irving, Washington. *The Western Journals of Washington Irving*, edited and annotated by John Francis McDermott. Norman: University of Oklahoma Press, 1944.

Keiser, Albert. *The Indian in American Literature.* New York: Oxford University Press, 1933, 52-64.

Kime, Wayne R. "Washington Irving and Frontier Speech." *American Speech*, XLII (February 1967), 5-18.

Kime, Wayne R. "Washington Irving's *Astoria:* A Critical Study." Unpublished doctoral dissertation, University of Delaware, 1968.

Kime, Wayne R. "Washington Irving's Revision of the *Tonquin* Episode in *Astoria.*" *Western American Literature*, IV (Spring 1969), 51-9.

Lee, Robert Edson. *From West to East.* Urbana: University of Illinois Press, 1966, 58-69.

Lyon, Thomas J. "Washington Irving's Wilderness." *Western American Literature*, I (Fall 1966), 167-74.

Martin, Terence. "Rip, Ichabod, and the American Imagination." *American Literature*, XXXI (1959), 137-49.

McDermott, John F. "Washington Irving and the Journal of Captain Bonneville." *Mississippi Valley Historical Review*, XLIII (December 1956), 459-67.

Myers, Andrew B. "Washington Irving, Fur Trade Chronicler: An Analysis of *Astoria* with Notes for a Corrected Edition." Unpublished doctoral dissertation, Columbia University, 1964.

Pochmann, Henry A. "Washington Irving." *Fifteen American Authors Before 1900: Bibliographic Essays on Research and Criticism.* Madison: University of Wisconsin Press, 1971.

Russell, Jason A. "Irving: Recorder of Indian Life." *Journal of American History*, XXV (1931), 185-95.

Short, Julee. "Irving's Eden: Oklahoma, 1832." *Journal of the West*, X (October 1971), 700-12.

Spaulding, George F., ed. *On the Western Tour with Washington Irving: The Journal and Letters of Count de Pourtales.* Translated by Seymour Feiler. Norman: University of Oklahoma Press, 1968.

Spaulding, Kenneth A. "A Note on *Astoria:* Irving's Use of the Robert Stuart Manuscript." *American Literature*, XXII (1950), 150-7.

Terrell, Dahlia Jewel. "A Textual Study of Washington Irving's *A Tour on the Prairies.*" Unpublished doctoral dissertation, University of Texas, 1966.

Thoburn, Joseph B. "Centennial of the Tour on the Prairies by Washington Irving." *Chronicles of Oklahoma*, X (September 1932), 426-33.

Todd, Edgeley W. "Washington Irving Discovers the Frontier." *Western Humanities Review*, XI (Winter 1957), 27-39.

Wagenknecht, Edward. *Washington Irving: Moderation Displayed.* New York: Oxford University Press, 1962.

Williams, Stanley T. *Life of Washington Irving.* 2 vols. New York: Oxford University Press, 1935.

Williams, Stanley T., and Mary A. Edge. *A Bibliography of the Writings of Washington Irving: A Check List.* New York: Oxford University Press, 1936.

Williams, Stanley T. and Barbara D. Simpson, eds. *Washington Irving on the Prairie, or, A Narrative of a Tour of the Southwest in the Year 1832.* New York: American Book Company, 1937.

HELEN HUNT JACKSON

Byers, John R., Jr. "Helen Hunt Jackson." *American Literary Realism 1870-1910*, II (Summer 1969), 143-8.

Dobie, J. Frank. "Helen Hunt Jackson and *Ramona.*" *Southwest Review*, XLIV (Spring 1959), 93-8.

Hamblen, Abigail Ann. "Ramona: A Story of Passion." *Western Review*, VIII (Spring 1971), 21-5.

Martin, Minerva L. "Helen Hunt Jackson, in Relation to Her Time." Unpublished doctoral dissertation, University of Louisiana, 1940.

Nevins, Allan. "Helen Hunt Jackson, Sentimentalist vs. Realist." *American Scholar*, X (1941), 269-85.

Odell, Ruth. *Helen Hunt Jackson.* New York: D. Appleton-Century Company, 1939.

Pound, Louise. "Biographical Accuracy and 'H. H.'" *American Literature*, II (January 1931), 418-21.

WILL JAMES

Amaral, Anthony. "A Dedication to the Memory of Will James, 1892-1942." *Arizona and the West*, X (Autumn 1968), 206-10.

Amaral, Anthony. *Will James: The Gilt Edged Cowboy.* Los Angeles: Westernlore Press, 1969.

ROBINSON JEFFERS

Adamic, Louis. *Robinson Jeffers, a Portrait.* Seattle: University of Washington Book Store, 1929.

Adams, John H. "The Poetry of Robinson Jeffers: Reinterpretation and Reevaluation." Unpublished doctroal dissertation, Denver University, 1967.

Alberts, S. S. *A Bibliography of the Works of Robinson Jeffers.* New York: Random House, 1933; Burt Franklin, 1968.

Antoninus, Brother. *Robinson Jeffers: Fragments of an Older Fury.* Berkeley: Oyez, 1968.

Beach, J. W. *The Concept of Nature in Nineteenth-Century English Poetry.* New York: Macmillan, 1936, 522-46.

Bennett, Melba B. *Robinson Jeffers and the Sea.* San Francisco: Belber, Lilenthal, Inc., 1936.

Bennett, Melba Berry. *The Stone Mason of Tor House: The Life and Work of Robinson Jeffers.* [Menlo Park, California]: The Ward Ritchie Press, 1966.

Boyers, Robert. "A Sovereign Voice: The Poetry of Robinson Jeffers." *Sewanee Review*, LXXVII (July-September 1969), 487-507.

Brophy, Robert J. "'Tamar,' 'The Cenci' and Incest." *American Literature*, XLII (May 1970), 241-4.

Brophy, Robert Joseph, S. J. "Structure, Symbol and Myth in Selected Narratives of Robinson Jeffers." Unpublished doctoral dissertation, University of North Carolina, 1966.

Carpenter, Frederic I. "Death Comes for Robinson Jeffers." *University Review*, VII (December 1940), 97-105.

Carpenter, Frederic I. *Robinson Jeffers.* New York: Twayne Publishers, 1962.

Carpenter, Frederic I. "Robinson Jeffers and the Torches of Violence." *The Twenties: Poetry and Prose*. Deland, Florida: Everett Edwards, 1966.

Carpenter, Frederic I. "The Values of Robinson Jeffers." *American Literature*, XI (January 1940), 353-66.

Cestre, Charles. "Robinson Jeffers." *Revue Ango-Américane*, IV (1927), 489-502.

Chatfield, Hale. "Robinson Jeffers: His Philosophy and His Major Themes." *Laurel Review*, VI (1966), 56-71.

Clark, Walter Van Tilburg. "A Study in Robinson Jeffers." Unpublished master's thesis, University of Vermont, 1934.

Coffin, Arthur B. *Robinson Jeffers*. Madison: University of Wisconsin Press, 1971.

Commanger, Henry Steele. "The Cult of the Irrational." *The American Mind*. New Haven: Yale University Press, 1950, 120-40.

Davis, Harold L. "Jeffers Denies Us Twice." *Poetry*, XXXI (1928), 274-9.

De Casseres, Benjamin. "Robinson Jeffers: Tragic Terror." *Bookman*, LXVI (November 1927), 262-6.

Deutsch, Babette. "A Look at the Worst." *Poetry in Our Time*. New York: Holt, 1952. 1-27.

Gierasch, Walter. "Robinson Jeffers." *English Journal* (College edition), XXVIII (April 1939), 284-95.

Gilbert, Rudolph. *Shine, Perishing Republic: Robinson Jeffers and the Tragic Sense in Modern Poetry*. Boston: Bruce Humphries, 1936.

Greenan, Edith. *Of Una Jeffers*. Los Angeles: Ward Ritchie Press, 1939.

Johnson, W. S. "The 'Savior' in the Poetry of Robinson Jeffers." *American Literature*, XV (May 1943), 159-68.

Keller, Karl. "California, Yankees, and the Death of God: The Allegory in Jeffers' *Roan Stallion*." *Texas Studies in Literature and Language*, XII (Spring 1970), 111-20.

Kiley, George B. "Robinson Jeffers: The Short Poems." Unpublished doctoral dissertation, University of Pittsburgh, 1957.

Macdonald, Dwight. "Robinson Jeffers." *Miscellany*, I (July, September 1930), 1-10, 1-24.

Monjian, Mercedes C. *Robinson Jeffers: A Study in Inhumanism*. Pittsburgh: University of Pittsburgh Press, 1958.

Morris, Lloyd S. "Robinson Jeffers: The Tragedy of a Modern Mystic." *The New Republic*, LIV (1928), 386-90.

Moss, Sidney P. "Robinson Jeffers: A Defense." *American Book Collector;* X (September 1959), 8-14.

Nolte, William H. *The Merrill Guide to Robinson Jeffers.* Columbus, Ohio: Charles E. Merrill Publishing Company, 1970.

Nolte, W. H. "Robinson Jeffers as Didactic Poet." *Virginia Quarterly Review,* XLII (Spring 1966), 257-71.

Powell, Lawrence Clark. "The Double Marriage of Robinson Jeffers." *Southwest Review,* XLI (Summer 1956), 278-82.

Powell, Lawrence Clark. *Robinson Jeffers: The Man and His Work.* Pasadena: San Pasqual Press, 1940.

Ridgeway, Ann N., ed. *The Selected Letters of Robinson Jeffers, 1897-1962.* Baltimore: The Johns Hopkins Press, 1968.

Robinson Jeffers: A Checklist. San Francisco: Gleeson Library Associates, 1967.

Robinson Jeffers Newsletter. Edited by Melba B. Bennett (nos. 1-22) and Robert J. Brophy (nos. 23-). Los Angeles: Robinson Jeffers Committee, Occidental College, 1962.

Schwartz, Delmore. "The Enigma of Robinson Jeffers: I. Sources of Violence." *Poetry,* LV (October 1939), 30-8.

Short, R. W. "The Tower Beyond Tragedy." *Southern Review,* VII (Summer 1941), 132-44.

Squires, Radcliffe. *The Loyalties of Robinson Jeffers.* Ann Arbor: University of Michigan Press, 1956.

Stephens, George D. "The Narrative and Dramatic Poetry of Robinson Jeffers." Unpublished doctoral dissertation, University of Southern California, 1953.

Sterling, George. *Robinson Jeffers, the Man and the Artist.* New York: Boni and Liveright, 1926.

Taylor, Frajan. "The Enigma of Robinson Jeffers: II The Hawk and the Stone." *Poetry,* LV (October 1939), 39-46.

Waggoner, Hyatt Howe. *The Heel of Elohim: Science and Values in Modern Poetry.* Norman: University of Oklahoma Press, 1950, 105-32.

Waggoner, Hyatt Howe. "Science and Poetry of Robinson Jeffers." *American Literature,* X (November 1938), 275-88.

Warren, R. P. "Jeffers on the Age." *Poetry,* XLIX (February 1937), 278-82.

Watts, H. H. "Multivalence in Robinson Jeffers." *College English,* III (November 1941), 109-20.

Watts, H. H. "Robinson Jeffers and Eating the Serpent." *Sewanee Review,* XLIX (January 1941), 39-55.

Weedin, Everett K., Jr. "Robinson Jeffers: The Achievement of His Narrative Verse." Unpublished doctoral dissertation, Cornell University, 1967.

White, William. "Robinson Jeffers: A Checklist, 1959-1965." *Serif,* III (June 1966), 36-9.

Wilder, Amos. "The Nihilism of Mr. Robinson Jeffers." *Spiritual Aspects of the New Poetry.* New York: Harper and Brothers, 1940, 141-52.

Winters, Yvor. "Robinson Jeffers." *Poetry* XXXV (February 1930), 279-86.

Woodbridge, H. C. "A Bibliographical Note on Jeffers." *American Book Collector,* X (September 1959), 15-8.

JACK KEROUAC

Charters, Ann. *A Bibliography of Work by Jack Kerouac.* New York: Phoenix Book Shop, 1967.

Cook, Bruce. *The Beat Generation.* New York: Charles Scribners, 1971.

Feied, Frederick. *No Pie in the Sky: The Hobo as American Cultural Hero in the Works of Jack London, John Dos Passos, and Jack Kerouac.* New York: Citadel, 1964.

Frohock, W. M. "Jack Kerouac and the Beats." *Strangers to This Ground.* Dallas: Southern Methodist University Press, 1961, 132-47.

"Jack Kerouac and Neal Cassady." *The Transatlantic Review,* XXXIII-XXXIV (Winter 1969-70), 115-25.

Leer, Norman. "Three American Novels and Contemporary Society." *Wisconsin Studies in Contemporary Literature,* III (Fall 1962), 67-86.

Rubin, Louis D. "Two Gentlemen of San Francisco: Notes on Kerouac and Responsibility." *Western Review,* XXIII (Spring 1959), 278-83.

Tallman, Warren. "Kerouac's Sound." *The Tamarack Review,* XI (Spring 1959), 58-74.

Webb, Howard W., Jr. "The Singular Worlds of Jack Kerouac." *Contemporary American Novelists,* Ed. Harry T. Moore. Carbondale: Southern Illinois University Press, 1964, 120-33.

KEN KESEY

Barsness, John A. "Ken Kesey: The Hero in Modern Dress." *Bulletin of the Rocky Mountain Language Association,* XXIII (March 1969), 27-33.

Billingsley, Ronald G. "The Artistry of Ken Kesey: A Study of *One Flew Over the Cuckoo's Nest* and of *Sometimes a Great Notion.*" Unpublished doctoral dissertation, University of Oregon, 1971.

Fiedler, Leslie. *The Return of the Vanishing American.* New York: Stein and Day, 1965, 159-87.

Hauck, Richard B. "The Comic Christ and the Modern Reader." *College English,* XXXI (February 1970), 498-506.

Kesey, Ken. "Letters from Mexico." in Jerome Charyn, ed. *The Single Voice: An Anthology of Contemporary Fiction.* London: Collier-Macmillan, Ltd., 1969, 417-26. Includes "An Introductory Note" by Ed McClanahan, 414-7.

Lish, Gordon, ed. "What the Hell You Looking in Here For, Daisy Mae: An Interview with Ken Kesey." *Genesis West,* II (Fall 1963), 17-29.

Olderman, Raymond Michael. "Beyond the Waste Land: A Study of the American Novel in the Nineteen-Sixties." Unpublished doctoral dissertation, Indiana University, 1969.

Sherwood, Terry G. "*One Flew Over the Cuckoo's Nest* and the Comic Strip." *Critique,* XIII (No. 1), 96-109.

Tanner, Tony. "Edge City: Ken Kesey and His Pranksters." *London Magazine,* IX (December 1969), 5-24.

Waldmeir, Joseph J. "Two Novelists of the Absurd: Heller and Kesey." *Wisconsin Studies in Contemporary Literature,* V (1964), 192-204.

Witke, Charles. "Pastoral Convention in Vergil and Kesey." *Pacific Coast Philology,* I (April 1966), 20-4.

Wolfe, Tom. *The Electric Kool-Aid Acid Test.* New York: Farrar, Straus and Giroux, Inc., 1968.

CHARLES KING

Burton, Wilfred C. "The Novels of Charles King, 1844-1933." Unpublished doctoral dissertation, New York University, 1962.

Peterson, Clell T. "Charles King: Soldier and Novelist." *American Book Collector,* XVI (December 1965), 9-12.

Sackett, S. J. "Captain Charles King, U.S.A." *Midwest Quarterly,* III (October 1961), 69-80.

JOSEPH KIRKLAND

Flanagan, John T. "Joseph Kirkland, Pioneer Realist." *American Literature,* XI (November 1939), 273-84.

Henson, Clyde E. "Joseph Kirkland (1830-1894)" *American Literary Realism 1870-1910,* I (Fall 1967), 67-70.

Henson, Clyde E. "Joseph Kirkland's Influence on Hamlin Garland." *American Literature,* XXIII (January 1952), 458-63.

Henson, Clyde E. *Joseph Kirkland.* New York: Twayne Publishers, 1962.

Holaday, Clayton A. "Joseph Kirkland: Biography and Criticism." Unpublished doctoral dissertation, Indiana University, 1950.

Lease, Benjamin. "Realism and Joseph Kirkland's *Zury.*" *American Literature*, XXIII (January 1952), 464-6.

CAROLYN KIZER

Howard, Richard. *Alone with America: Essays on the Art of Poetry in the United States Since 1950.* New York: Atheneum, 1969, pp. 272-80.

HERBERT KRAUSE

Janssen, Judith M. " 'Black Frost in Summer': Central Themes in the Novels of Herbert Krause." *South Dakota Review*, V (Spring 1967), 55-65.

PETER B. KYNE

Bode, Carl. "Cappy Ricks and the Monk in the Garden." *PMLA*, LXIV (March 1949), 59-69.

OLIVER LaFARGE

Allen, Charles. "The Fiction of Oliver LaFarge." *Arizona Quarterly*, I (Winter 1945), 74-81.

Brokaw, Zoanne S. "Oliver LaFarge: His Fictional Navajo." Unpublished master's thesis, University of Arizona, 1965.

Bunker, Robert. "Oliver LaFarge: The Search for Self." *New Mexico Quarterly*, XX (1950), 211-24.

Gillis, Everett A. *Oliver LaFarge.* Southwest Writers Series, No. 9. Austin, Texas: Steck-Vaughn Company, 1967.

McHenry, Carol S. "Tradition: Ballast in Transition; A Literary Biography of Oliver LaFarge." Unpublished doctor's thesis, University of New Mexico, 1966.

McNickle, D'. Arcy. *Indian Man: A Life of Oliver LaFarge.* Bloomington: Indiana University Press, 1971.

Scott, Winfield Townley. "Introduction." in Oliver LaFarge. *The Man with the Calabash Pipe.* Boston: Houghton Mifflin Company, 1966, xi-xxi.

LOUIS L'AMOUR

Walker, Don D. "Notes on the Popular Western." *The Possible Sack* [University of Utah], III (November 1971), 11-3.

JOHN S. LANGRISCHE

Cochran, Alice C. "John S. Langrische and the Theater of the Mining Frontier." Unpublished master's thesis, Southern Methodist University, 1969.

CLINTON F. LARSON

"A Conversation with Clinton F. Larson." *Dialogue: A Journal of Mormon Thought*, IV (Autumn 1969), 74-80.

D. H. LAWRENCE

Foster, Joseph. *D. H. Lawrence in Taos.* Albuquerque: University of New Mexico Press, 1971.

Halperin, Irving. "Unity in *St. Mawr.*" *South Dakota Review*, IV (Summer 1966), 58-60.

Merrild, Knud. *With D. H. Lawrence in New Mexico: A Memoir of D. H. Lawrence.* New York: Barnes and Noble, 1965.

Smith, Bob L. "D. H. Lawrence's *St. Mawr:* Transposition of a Myth." *Arizona Quarterly*, XXIV (Autumn 1968), 197-208.

Waters, Frank. "Quetzalcoatl Versus D. H. Lawrence's *Plumed Serpent.*" *Western American Literature*, III (Summer 1968), 103-13.

TOM LEA

Braddy, Haldeen. "Artist Illustrators of the Southwest: H. D. Bugbee, Tom Lea and Jose Cisneros." *Western Review*, I (Fall 1964), 37-41.

Bromfield, Louis. "Triumphs in the Arena." *Saturday Review of Literature*, XXXII (April 23, 1949), 10-2.

Dykes, Jeff C. "Tentative Bibliographic Check Lists of Western Illustrators." *American Book Collector*, XV (April 1965), 25-32.

West, John O. *Tom Lea, Artist in Two Mediums.* Southwest Writers Series, No. 5. Austin: Steck-Vaughn Company, 1967.

ALFRED HENRY LEWIS

Boyer, M. G., ed. *Arizona in Literature*. Glendale, California, 1934.

Filler, Louis. "The West Belongs to All of Us." *Old Wolfville: Chapters from the Fiction of Alfred Henry Lewis*. Yellow Springs, Ohio: The Antioch Press, 1968, vii-xii.

Filler, Louis. "Wolfville." *New Mexico Quarterly Review*, XIII (Spring 1943), 35-47.

Herron, Ima Honaker. *The Small Town in American Literature*. Durham: University Press, 1939, 280-2.

Humphries, Rolfe. "Introduction." *Wolfville Yarns of Alfred Henry Lewis*. [Kent, Ohio]: The Kent State University Press, 1968, v-xviii.

Manzo, Flournoy D. "Alfred Henry Lewis: Western Story Teller." *Arizona and the West*, X (Spring 1968), 5-24.

Manzo, Flournoy Davis. "Alfred Henry Lewis: Western Story Teller." Unpublished master's thesis, Texas Western College, 1966.

Turner, Tressa. "The Life and Works of Alfred Henry Lewis." Unpublished master's thesis, University of Texas, 1936.

JAMES FRANKLIN LEWIS

Lund, Mary Graham. "James Franklin Lewis, Transhumanist." *The University Review*, XXXIII (June 1967), 307-12.

JANET LEWIS

Davie, Donald. "The Historical Narratives of Janet Lewis." *Southern Review*, New Series II (Winter 1966), 40-60.

Inglis, Fred. "The Novels of Janet Lewis." *Critique*, VII (1965), 47-64.

Swallow, Alan. "The Mavericks." *Critique* II (Winter 1959), 77-9.

MERIWETHER LEWIS
(Lewis and Clark)

Bakeless, John E. *Lewis and Clark: Partners in Discovery*. New York: William Morrow, 1947.

Bewley, Marius. "The Heroic and the Romantic West." *Masks and Mirrors*. New York: Atheneum, 1970, 213-20.

Criswell, Elijah H. *Lewis and Clark: Linguistic Pioneers*. Columbia: University of Missouri, 1940.

DeVoto, Bernard, ed. *The Journals of Lewis and Clark*. Boston: Houghton Mifflin Company, 1953.

Dillon, Richard. *Meriwether Lewis: A Biography*. New York: Coward-McCann, 1965.

Jackson, Donald, ed. *Letters of the Lewis and Clark Expedition with Related Documents, 1783-1854*. Urbana: University of Illinois Press, 1962.

Lee, Robert Edson. *From West to East*. Urbana: University of Illinois Press, 1966, 11-38.

Stevenson, Elizabeth. "Meriwether and I." *Virginia Quarterly Review*, XLIII (Autumn 1967), 580-91.

Thwaites, Reuben Gold, ed. *Original Journals of the Lewis and Clark Expedition, 1804-1806*. 8 vols. New York: Dodd, Mead and Company, 1904-5.

SINCLAIR LEWIS

Baker, Joseph E. "Sinclair Lewis, Plato, and the Regional Escape." *English Journal* (College edition), XXVIII (June 1939), 460-72.

Bucco, Martin. "The Serialized Novels of Sinclair Lewis." *Western American Literature*, IV (Spring 1969), 29-37.

DeVoto, Bernard. *The Literary Fallacy*. Boston: Little, Brown and Company, 1944, 95-123.

Dooley, D. J. *The Art of Sinclair Lewis*. Lincoln: University of Nebraska Press, 1967.

Fife, Jim L. "Two Views of the American West." *Western American Literature*, I (Spring 1966), 34-43.

Flanagan, John T. "A Long Way to Gopher Prairie: Sinclair Lewis's Apprenticeship." *Southwest Review*, XXXII (Autumn 1947), 403-13.

Flanagan, John T. "The Minnesota Backgrounds of Sinclair Lewis's Fiction." *Minnesota History*, XXXVII (March 1960), 1-13.

From Main Street to Stockholm: Letters of Sinclair Lewis, 1919-1930, edited by and with introduction by Harrison Smith. New York: Harcourt, Brace and Company, 1952.

Geismar, Maxwell. *The Last of the Provincials: The American Novel, 1915-1925*. Boston: Houghton Mifflin Company, 1947, 69-150.

Grebstein, Sheldon Norman. *Sinclair Lewis*. New York: Twayne, 1962.

Grebstein, Sheldon. "Sinclair Lewis' Minnesota Boyhood." *Minnesota History*, XXXIV (Autumn 1954), 85-9.

Hartwick, Harry. "The Village Virus." *The Foreground of American Fiction.* New York: American Book Company, 1934, 250-81.

Hilfer, Anthony Channell. *The Revolt from the Village.* Chapel Hill: University of North Carolina Press, 1969, 158-92.

Horton, T. D. "Sinclair Lewis: The Symbol of an Era." *North American Review,* CCXLVIII (Winter 1939), 374-93.

Lewis, Grace Hegger. *With Love from Gracie.* New York: Harcourt, Brace, 1955.

Lundquist, James. *The Merrill Checklist of Sinclair Lewis.* Columbus: Charles E. Merrill Publishing Company, 1970.

Lundquist, James. *The Merrill Guide to Sinclair Lewis.* Columbus: Charles E. Merrill Publishing Company, 1970.

Lundquist, James, ed. *Sinclair Lewis Newsletter.* I (1969—), St. Cloud State College [Minnesota].

Schorer, Mark. *Sinclair Lewis.* University of Minnesota Pamphlets on American Writers. Minneapolis: University of Minnesota, 1963.

Schorer, Mark, ed. *Sinclair Lewis: A Collection of Critical Essays.* Englewood Cliffs, N. J.: Prentice-Hall, 1962.

Schorer, Mark. *Sinclair Lewis: An American Life.* New York: McGraw-Hill, 1961.

Sheean, Vincent. *Dorothy and Red.* Bofton: Houghton Mifflin Company, 1963.

Sheean, Vincent. "The Tangled Romance of Sinclair Lewis and Dorothy Thompson." *Harper's,* CCXXVII (October 1963), 121-72.

South Dakota Review, VII (Winter 1969-70), 3-78.

Thompson, Dorothy. "The Boy and Man from Sauk Centre." *Atlantic,* CCVI (November 1960), 39-48.

FRANK B. LINDERMAN

Merriam, H. G. "The Life and Work of Frank B. Linderman." *Montana Adventure: The Recollections of Frank B. Linderman.* Lincoln: University of Nebraska, 1968, 199-214.

Merriam, Harold G. "Sign-Talker with Straight Tongue: Frank Bird Linderman." *Montana,* XII (Summer 1962), 2-20.

Smith, Jean P. "Frank B. Linderman: Sign Talker." *Frontier,* XI (November 1930), 59 ff.

Van de Water, F. F. "The Work of Frank B. Linderman." *Frontier and Midland,* XIX (Spring 1939), 148-52.

VACHEL LINDSAY

Avery, Emmett L. "Vachel Lindsay: Spokane Journalist." *Research Studies of the State College of Washington*, XXV (March 1957), 101-10.

Avery, Emmett L. "Vachel Lindsay in Spokane." *Pacific Spectator*, III (1949), 338-53.

Avery, Emmett L. "Vachel Lindsay's 'Poem Games' in Spokane." *Research Studies of Washington State University*, XXX (Summer 1962), 109-14.

Gilliland, Marshall A. "Vachel Lindsay: Poet and Newspaper Columnist in Spokane, 1924-1929." Unpublished doctoral dissertation, Washington State University, 1968.

Massa, Ann. *Vachel Lindsay: Fieldworker for the American Dream.* Bloomington: Indiana University Press, 1970.

Ruggles, Eleanor. *The West-Going Heart: A Life of Vachel Lindsay.* New York: W. W. Norton and Company, 1959.

Trombly, A. E. "Listeners and Readers: The Unforgetting of Vachel Lindsay." *Southwest Review*, XLVII (August 1962), 294-302.

JACK LONDON

Baskett, Sam S. "Jack London on the Oakland Waterfront." *American Literature*, XXVII (1955), 363-71.

Baskett, Sam S. "Jack London's Heart of Darkness." *American Quarterly*, X (Spring 1958), 66-77.

Benoit, Raymond. "Jack London's *The Call of the Wild.*" *American Quarterly*, XX (Summer 1968), 246-8.

Ellis, James. "A Reading of *The Sea Wolf.*" *Western American Literature*, II (Summer 1967), 127-34.

Erbentrant, Edwin B. "The Intellectual Undertow in *Martin Eden.*" *Jack London Newsletter*, III (January-April 1970), 12-24.

Findley, Sue. "Naturalism in 'To Build a Fire.' " *Jack London Newsletter*, II (May-August 1969), 45-8.

Foner, Philip S. *Jack London: American Rebel.* New York: Citadel, 1947, 1964.

Geismar, Maxwell. *Rebels and Ancestors: The American Novel, 1890-1915.* Boston, 1953, 139-216.

Gurian, Jay. "The Romantic Necessity in Literary Naturalism: Jack London." *American Literature*, XXXVIII (March 1966), 112-20.

Haydock, James. "Jack London: A Bibliography of Criticism." *Bulletin of Bibliography*, XXIII (May-August 1960), 42-6.

Hendricks, King. *Jack London: Master Craftsman of the Short Story*. Logan, Utah: Utah State University, 1966.

Hendricks, King, and Irving Shepard, eds. *Letters from Jack London, Containing an Unpublished Correspondence between London and Sinclair Lewis*. New York: Odyssey, 1965.

Jennings, Ann S. "London's Code of the Northland." *Alaska Review*, I (Fall 1964), 43-8.

Labor, Earle. "Jack London's Symbolic Wilderness: Four Versions." *Nineteenth-Century Fiction*, XVII (Summer 1962), 149-61.

London, Charmian. *The Book of Jack London*. 2 vols. New York: Century, 1921.

London, Joan. *Jack London and His Times: An Unconventional Biography*. New York: Doubleday, Doran, 1939; Seattle: University of Washington, 1968.

Lynn, Kenneth S. *The Dream of Success*. Boston, 1955, 75-118.

McClintock, James I. "Jack London's Use of Carl Jung's *Psychology of the Unconscious*." *American Literature*, LXII (November 1970), 336-47.

Mills, Gordon. "Jack London's Quest for Salvation." *American Quarterly*, Vii (Spring 1955), 3-14.

Mills, Gordon. "The Symbolic Wilderness: James Fenimore Cooper and Jack London." *Nineteenth Century Fiction*, XIII (March 1959), 329-40.

Nichol, John. "The Role of 'Local Color' in Jack London's Alaska Wilderness Tales." *Western Review*, VI (Winter 1969), 51-6.

O'Connor, Richard. *Jack London: A Biography*. Boston: Little, Brown, 1964.

Pearsall, Robert Brainard. "Elizabeth Barrett Meets Wolf Larsen." *Western American Literature*, IV (Spring 1969), 3-13.

Peterson, Clell T. "Jack London's Sonoma Novels." *American Book Collector*, IX (October 1958), 15-20.

Peterson, Clell T. "The Theme of Jack London's 'To Build a Fire.' " *American Book Collector*, XVII (November 1966), 15-8.

Price, Starling. "Jack London's America." Unpublished doctoral dissertation, University of Minnesota, 1970.

Shivers, Alfred S. "Jack London: Not a Suicide." *Dalhousie Review*, XLIX (Spring 1969), 43-57.

Shivers, Alfred S. "The Romantic in Jack London: Far Away from Frozen Places." *Alaskan Review*, I (Winter 1963), 38-47.

Stone, Irving. *Sailor on Horseback: The Biography of Jack London*. Boston: Houghton Mifflin, 1938.

Vanderbeets, Richard. "Nietzsche of the North: Heredity and Race in London's *The Son of the Wolf*." *Western American Literature*, II (Fall 1967), 229-33.

Walcutt, Charles Child. *American Literary Naturalism, A Divided Stream.* Minneapolis: University of Minnesota Press, 1956, 87-113.

Walcutt, Charles Child. *Jack London.* University of Minnesota pamphlets on American Writers, No. 57. Minneapolis: University of Minnesota Press, 1966.

Walker, Dale L. "Jack London (1876-1916)." *American Literary Realism 1870-1910,* I (Fall 1967), 71-8.

Walker, Franklin. *Jack London and the Klondike. San Marino: The Huntington Library, 1966.*

Walker, Franklin. "Jack London, *Martin Eden.*" *The American Novel from James Fenimore Cooper to William Faulkner,* ed. Wallace Stegner. New York: Basic Books, 1965.

Walker, Franklin. "Jack London's Use of Sinclair Lewis Plots, Together with a Printing of Three of the Plots." *Huntington Library Quarterly,* XVII (November 1953), 59-74.

Warner, Richard H. "A Contemporary Sketch of Jack London." *American Literature,* XXXVIII (November 1966), 376-80.

Wilcox, Earl J. "Jack London and the Tradition of American Literary Naturalism." Unpublished doctoral dissertation, Vanderbilt University, 1966.

Wilcox, Earl J. "Jack London's Naturalism: The Example of *The Call of the Wild.*" *Jack London Newsletter,* II (September-December 1969), 91-101.

Wilcox, Earl J. "Le Milieu, Le Moment, La Race: Literary Naturalism in Jack London's *White Fang.*" *Jack London Newsletter,* III (May-August 1970), 42-55.

Woodbridge, Hensley C. "Jack London: A Bibliography (A Supplement)." *American Book Collector,* XVII (November 1966), 32-5.

Woodbridge, Hensley C. *Jack London Newsletter.* Carbondale: Southern Illinois University Library.

Woodbridge, Hensley C., John London, and George H. Tweney. *Jack London: A Bibliography.* Georgetown: Talisman Press, 1966.

MABEL DODGE LUHAN

Brett, Dorothy E. "Autobiography: My Long and Beautiful Journey." *South Dakota Review,* V (Summer 1967), 11-71.

Morrill, Claire. "Three Women of Taos: Frieda Lawrence, Mabel Luhan, and Dorothy Brett." *South Dakota Review,* II (Spring 1965), 3-22.

CHARLES FLETCHER LUMMIS

Bingham, Edwin. *Charles F. Lummis: Editor of the Southwest.* San Marino: The Huntington Library, 1955.

Gordon, Dudley C. "Charles F. Lummis: Pioneer American Folklorist." *Western Folklore,* XXVIII (July 1969), 175-81.

Gordon, Dudley. "Charles Fletcher Lummis, Cultural Pioneer of the Southwest." *Arizona and the West,* I (Winter 1959), 305-16.

Newmark, Marco. "Charles Fletcher Lummis." *Historical Society of Southern California Quarterly,* XXXII (March 1950), 45-60.

GILES LUTZ

Etulain, Richard. "Recent Western Fiction." *Journal of the West,* VIII (October 1969), 656-8.

HARRIS MERTON LYON

Lyon, Zoë. "Harris Merton Lyon: Early American Realist." *Studies in Short Fiction,* V (Summer 1968), 368-77.

NORMAN MAILER

Witt, Grace. "The Bad Man as Hipster: Norman Mailer's Use of Frontier Metaphor." *Western American Literature,* IV (Fall 1969), 202-17.

BERNARD MALAMUD

Barsness, John A. *"A New Life:* The Frontier Myth in Perspective." *Western American Literature,* III (Winter 1969), 297-302.

Hollander, John. "To Find the Westward Path." *Partisan Review,* XXIX (Winter 1962), 137-9.

Richman, Sidney. *Bernard Malamud.* New York: Twayne Publishers, 1966, 78-97.

Schulz, Max F. "Malamud's *A New Life:* The New Wasteland of the Fifties." *Western Review,* VI (Summer 1969), 37-44.

Solotaroff, Theodore. "Bernard Malamud's Fiction: The Old Life and the New." *Commentary,* XXX (March 1962), 197-204.

FREDERICK FEIKEMA MANFRED

Austin, James C. "Legend, Myth and Symbol in Frederick Manfred's *Lord Grizzly." Critique*, VI (Winter 1963-64), 122-30.

Bebeau, Don. "A Search for Voice: A Sense of Place in *The Golden Bowl." South Dakota Review*, VII (Winter 1969-70), 79-86.

Kellogg, George. "Frederick Manfred: A Bibliography." *Twentieth Century Literature*, XI (April 1965), 30-5.

Michael, Larry A. "Literary Allusions in the Fiction of Frederick Manfred." Unpublished master's thesis, University of South Dakota, 1965.

Milton, John R. "Frederick Feikema Manfred." *Western Review*, XXII (Spring 1958), 181-98.

Milton, John R. "Interview with Frederick Manfred." *South Dakota Review*, VII (Winter 1969-70), 110-30.

Milton, John R. *"Lord Grizzly:* Rhythm, Form and Meaning in the Western Novel." *Western American Literature*, I (Spring 1966), 6-14.

Milton, John R. "Voice from Siouxland: Frederick Feikema Manfred." *College English*, XIX (December 1957), 104-11.

Peet, Howard. "Evolution of a Man Named Fred." Unpublished master's thesis, Moorhead State College, 1965.

Roth, Russell. "The Inception of a Saga: Frederick Manfred's 'Buckskin Man.' " *South Dakota Review*, VII (Winter 1969-70), 87-99.

Swallow, Alan. "The Mavericks." *Critique* II (Winter 1959), 88-92.

"West of the Mississippi: An Interview with Frederick Manfred." *Critique*, II (Winter 1959), 35-56.

Wylder, D. E. "Manfred's Indian Novel." *South Dakota Review*, VII (Winter 1969-70), 100-9.

EDWIN MARKHAM

Arlt, G. O. "Poet Laureate: Edwin Markham." *Historical Society of Southern California Quarterly*, XXXIV (September 1952), 199-212.

Clemens, Cyril, *et.al.* "Edwin Markham Number." *Mark Twain Quarterly*, IV (Spring 1941), 1-20.

Filler, Louis. "Edwin Markham, Poetry and What Have You." *Antioch Review*, XXIII (1963), 447-59.

Filler, Louis. *The Unknown Edwin Markham: His Mystery and Its Significance.* Yellow Springs, Ohio: Antioch Press, 1966.

Goldstein, Jessie S. "Edwin Markham, Ambrose Bierce, and 'The Man with the Hoe.' " *Modern Language Notes*, LVIII (March 1943), 165-75.

Goldstein, Jessie. "Escapade of a Poet." *Pacific Historical Review,* XIII (September 1944), 303-13.

Goldstein, Jessie. "Life of Edwin Markham." Unpublished doctoral dissertation, New York University, 1945.

Grose, G. R. "Edwin Markham: Poet of the Social Conscience." *Personalist,* XVII (April 1936), 149-56.

Synnestvedt, Sigfried T. "Bread, Beauty, and Brotherhood: The Ethical Consciousness of Edwin Markham." Unpublished doctoral dissertation, University of Pennsylvania, 1959.

ALICE MARRIOTT

Kobler, Turner S. *Alice Marriott.* Southwest Writers Series, No. 27.Austin, Texas: Steck-Vaughn Company, 1969.

TOM MAYER

Davis, Kenneth W. "The Theme of Initiation in the Works of Larry McMurtry and Tom Mayer." *The Arlington Quarterly,* II (Winter 1969), 29-43.

MICHAEL McCLURE

Clements, Marshall. *A Catalog of Works by Michael McClure.* New York: Phoenix Book Shop, 1965.

LARRY McMURTRY

Clemons, Walter. "The Last Word: An Overlooked Novel." *New York Times Book Review,* (August 15, 1971), 39.

Davis, Kenneth W. "The Themes of Initiation in the Work of Larry McMurtry and Tom Mayer." *The Arlington Quarterly,* II (Winter 1969-70), 29-43.

Landess, Thomas. *Larry McMurtry.* Southwest Writers Series, No. 23. Austin, Texas: Steck-Vaughn Company, 1969.

Peavy, Charles D. "Coming of Age in Texas: The Novels of Larry McMurtry." *Western American Literature,* IV (Fall 1969), 171-88.

Peavy, Charles D. "A Larry McMurtry Bibliography." *Western American Literature,* III (Fall 1968), 235-48.

Peavy, Charles D. "Larry McMurtry and Black Humor: A Note on *The Last Picture Show.*" *Western American Literature,* II (Fall 1969), 223-7.

Pilkington, William T. "The Dirt Farmer and the Cowboy: Notes on Two Texas Essayists." *RE: Arts and Letters,* III (Fall 1969), 42-54.

Sonnichsen, C. L. "The New Style Western." *South Dakota Review,* IV (Summer 1966), 22-8.

CHARLES L. McNICHOLS

Berner, Robert L. "Charles L. McNichols and *Crazy Weather:* A Reconsideration." *Western American Literature,* VI (Spring 1971), 39-51.

GEORGE MILBURN

Herron, Ima Honaker. *The Small Town in American Literature.* Durham: Duke University Press, 1939.

Turner, Steven. *George Milburn.* Southwest Writers Series, No. 28. Austin, Texas: Steck-Vaughn Company, 1970.

JOAQUIN MILLER

Beebe, Beatrice B., ed. "Letters of Joaquin Miller." *Frontier,* XII (1932), 121-4, 223-8, 344-7.

Brendemuhl, Gavriella C. "Joaquin Miller's Indebtedness to Byron in Connection with His Early Narrative Poems." Unpublished doctoral dissertation, University of Chicago, 1921.

Buchanan, L. E. "Joaquin Miller in the Passing of the Old West." *Research Studies of Washington State University,* XXXII (1964), 326-33.

Duckett, Margaret. "Carlyle, 'Columbus,' and Joaquin Miller." *Philological Quarterly,* XXXV (1956), 443-7.

Dunbar, John Raine. "Joaquin Miller: Sedition and Civil War." *Pacific Historical Review,* XIX (1950), 31-6.

Dykes, Mattie M. "Joaquin Miller: A Biographical Study." Unpublished doctoral dissertation, University of Chicago, 1922.

Frost, O. W. *Joaquin Miller.* New York: Twayne Publishers, Inc. 1967.

Haight, Mary M. "Joaquin Miller in Oregon, 1852-54 and 1857-70." Unpublished doctoral disseration, University of Washington, 1936.

Marberry, M. Marion. *Splendid Poseur: Joaquin Miller—American Poet.* New York: Thomas Y. Crowell, 1953.

Peterson, Martin Severin. *Joaquin Miller: Literary Frontiersman.* Palo Alto: Stanford University Press, 1937.

Powers, Alfred. *History of Oregon Literature.* Portland: Metropolitan Press, 1935.

Reade, Frank R. "Cincinnatus Hiner Miller: A Critical Biography." Unpublished doctoral dissertation, University of Virginia, 1926.

Richards, John S., ed. *Joaquin Miller: His California Diary.* Seattle: F. McCaffrey, 1936.

Sherman, Stuart P., ed. *The Poetical Works of Joaquin Miller.* New York: G. P. Putnam, 1923.

Thompson, H. C. "Reminiscences of Joaquin Miller and Canyon City." *Oregon Historical Quarterly,* XLV (1944), 326-36.

Wagner, Harr. *Joaquin Miller and His Other Self.* San Francisco: Harr Wagner, 1929.

Walker, Franklin. *San Francisco's Literary Frontier.* New York: Alfred A. Knopf, 1939.

Walterhouse, Roger R. "Bret Harte, Joaquin Miller, and the Western Local Color Story." Unpublished doctoral dissertation, University of Chicago, 1936.

N. SCOTT MOMADAY

Contemporary Authors. Vols. 25-28. Detroit: Gale Research Company, 1971, 520.

Haslam, Gerald W. *Forgotten Pages of American Literature.* Boston: Houghton Mifflin Company, 1970, 13-28.

Winters, Yvor. *Forms of Discovery.* Alan Swallow, 1967, 279-84.

WRIGHT MORRIS

Baumbach, Jonathan. "Wake Before Bomb: *Ceremony in Lone Tree.*"IV, *Critique* (Winter 1961-62), 56-71.

Bleufarb, Sam. "Point of View: An Interview with Wright Morris." *Accent,* XIX (Winter 1959), 34-46.

Booth, Wayne C. "The Shaping of Prophecy: Craft and Idea in the Novels of Wright Morris." *The American Scholar,* XXXI (Autumn 1962), 608-26.

Booth, Wayne C. "The Two Worlds in the Fiction of Wright Morris." *Sewanee Review*, LXV (Summer 1957), 375-99.

Brenner, Jack. "Wright Morris: A Novelist's View of American Character." Unpublished doctoral dissertation, University of New Mexico, 1970.

Carpenter, Frederic I. "Wright Morris and the Territory Ahead." *College English*, XXI (December 1959), 147-56.

Crump, Gail Bruce. "Wright Morris and the Immediate Present." Unpublished doctoral dissertation, University of Arkansas, 1970.

Eisinger, Chester E. *Fiction of the Forties*. Chicago: University of Chicago Press, 1963, 328-41.

Flanagan, John T. "The Fiction of Wright Morris." *Studia Germanica Gandensia*, III (1961), 209-31.

Garrett, George. "Morris The Magician: A Look at *In Orbit*." *Hollins Critic*, IV (June 1967), 1-12.

Guettinger, Roger J. "The Problem with Jigsaw Puzzles: Form in the Fiction of Wright Morris." *Texas Quarterly*, XI (Spring 1968), 209-20.

Hicks, Granville, ed. with Introduction. *Wright Morris: A Reader*. New York: Harper and Row, 1970.

Howard, Leon. *Wright Morris*. Minneapolis: University of Minnesota, 1968.

Hunt, John W., Jr. "The Journey Back: The Early Novels of Wright Morris." *Critique*, V (Spring-Summer 1962), 41-60.

Klein, Marcus. *After Alienation*. New York: The World Publishing Company, 1964, 196-246.

Linden, Stanton J., and David Madden. "A Wright Morris Bibliography." *Critique*, IV (Winter 1961-62), 77-87.

Madden, David. "The Hero and the Witness in Wright Morris' Field of Vision." *Prairie Schooner*, XXXIV (Fall 1960), 263-78.

Madden, David. "The Great Plains in the Novels of Wright Morris." *Critique*, IV (Winter 1961-62), 5-23.

Madden, David. *Wright Morris*. New York: Twayne Publishers, 1964.

Madden, David, *et al.* "Wright Morris Issue." *Critique*, IV (Winter 1961-62), 5-87.

Miller, James E., Jr. "The Nebraska Encounter: Willa Cather and Wright Morris." *Prairie Schooner*, XLI (Summer 1967), 165-7.

Morris, Wright. "Introduction: A Case for Thanks." *Themes and Directions in American Literature: Essays in Honor of Leon Howard*, eds. Ray B. Browne and Donald Pizer. Purdue University Studies. Lafayette, Indiana: Purdue University Press, 1969, 2-5.

Morris, Wright. *The Territory Ahead*. New York: Harcourt, Brace, 1958.

Shetty, M. Nalini. "The Fiction of Wright Morris." Unpublished doctoral dissertation, University of Pittsburgh, 1967.

Shetty, Nalini V. "Wright Morris and the Territory Ahead." *Indian Essays in American Literature*. Bombay: Popular Prakashan, 1969, 71-83.

Trachtenberg, Alan. "The Craft of Vision." *Critique*, IV (Winter 1961-62), 41-55.

Tucker, Martin. "The Landscape of Wright Morris." *Lock Haven Review*, VII (1965), 43-51.

Waldeland, Lynne Marit. "Wright Morris: His Theory and Practice of the Craft of Fiction." Unpublished doctoral dissertation, Purdue University, 1970.

Waterman, Arthur E. "The Novels of Wright Morris: An Escape from Nostalgia." *Critique*, IV (Winter 1961-62), 24-40.

JOHN MUIR

Badé, William F. *The Life and Letters of John Muir.* Boston: Houghton Mifflin Company, 1924.

Colby, William E., ed. *Studies in the Sierra.* San Francisco: The Sierra Club, 1950.

Cosbey, Robert C. "John Muir." Unpublished doctoral dissertation, Ohio State University, 1949.

Hadley, Edith. "John Muir's Views of Nature and Their Consequences." Unpublished doctoral dissertation, University of Wisconsin, 1956.

Smith, Herbert F. *John Muir.* New York: Twayne Publishers, 1965.

Teale, Edwin Way, ed. *The Wilderness World of John Muir.* Boston: Houghton Mifflin Company, 1954.

Weber, Daniel B. "John Muir: The Function of Wilderness in an Industrial Society." Unpublished doctoral dissertation, University of Minnesota, 1964.

Wolfe, Linnie Marsh, ed. *John of the Mountains: The Unpublished Journals of John Muir.* Boston: Houghton Mifflin Company, 1938.

Wolfe, Linnie Marsh. *Son of the Wilderness: The Life of John Muir.* Boston: Houghton Mifflin Company, 1954.

CLARENCE MULFORD

Durham, Philip. "Jay Gatsby and Hopalong Cassidy." *Themes and Directions in American Literature: Essays in Honor of Leon Howard*, eds. Ray B. Browne and Donald Pizer. Purdue University Studies. Lafayette, Indiana: Purdue University Press, 1969, 163-70.

Jensen, Oliver. "Hopalong Hits the Jackpot." *Life*, (June 12, 1950), 63-70.

Perham, Joseph A. "Reflections on Hopalong Cassidy: A Study of Clarence E. Mulford." Unpublished master's thesis, University of Maine, 1966.

JOHN G. NEIHARDT

Adkins, Nelson F. "A Study of John G. Neihardt's 'Song of Three Friends.' " *American Speech*, III (April 1928), 276-90.

Aly, Lucile F. "John G. Neihardt as Speaker and Reader." Unpublished doctoral dissertation, University of Missouri, 1959.

Aly, Lucile F. "The Word-Sender: John G. Neihardt and His Audiences." *Quarterly Journal of Speech*, XLIII (April 1957), 151-4.

Black, W. E. "Ethic and Metaphysic: A Study of John G. Neihardt." *Western American Literature*, II (Fall 1967), 205-12.

Flanagan, John T. "John G. Neihardt, Chronicler of the West." *Arizona Quarterly*, XXI(Spring 1965), 7-20.

Grant, George Paul. "The Poetic Development of John G. Neihardt." Unpublished doctoral dissertation, University of Pittsburgh, 1958.

House, Julian T. *John G. Neihardt, Man and Poet*. Wayne, Nebraska, 1920.

Kay, Arthur Murray. "The Epic Intent and the American Dream: The Westering Theme in Modern American Narrative Poetry." Unpublished doctoral dissertation, Columbia University, 1961, 158-84.

Rothwell, Kenneth S. "In Search of a Western Epic: Neidhardt, Sandburg and Jaffe as Regionalists and 'Astoriadists.' " *Kansas Quarterly*, II (Spring 1970), 53-63.

Slote, Bernice D. "Neihardt: Nebraska's Poet Laureate." *Prairie Schooner*, XLI (Summer 1967), 178-81.

Todd, Edgeley W. "The Frontier Epic: Frank Norris and John G. Neihardt." *Western Humanities Review*, XIII (Winter 1959), 40-5.

CHARLES NORRIS

Goldsmith, Arnold L. "Charles and Frank Norris." *Western American Literature*, II (Spring 1967), 30-49.

FRANK NORRIS

Ahnebrink, Lars. *The Beginnings of Naturalism in American Fiction.* Upsala: Upsala University Press, 1950.

Bixler, Paul H. "Frank Norris's Literary Reputation." *American Literature*, VI (May 1934), 109-21.

Chase, Richard. *The American Novel and Its Tradition.* Garden City: Doubleday, 1957, 185-204.

Cooperman, Stanley. "Frank Norris and the Werewolf of Guilt." *Modern Language Quarterly*, XX (1959), 252-8.

Dillingham, William B. "Frank Norris." *Fifteen American Authors Before 1900: Bibliographic Essays on Research and Criticism.* Madison: University of Wisconsin Press, 1971.

Dillingham, William B. "Frank Norris and the Genteel Tradition." *Tennessee Studies in Literature*, V (1960), 15-24.

Dillingham, William B. *Frank Norris: Instinct and Art.* Lincoln: University of Nebraska Press, 1969; Boston: Houghton Mifflin Company, 1969.

Folsom, James K. "Social Darwinism or Social Protest? The 'Philosophy' of *The Octopus.*" *Modern Fiction Studies*, VII (Winter 1962-63), 393-400.

French, Warren. *Frank Norris.* New York: Twayne, 1962.

French, Warren. "Frank Norris (1870-1902)." *American Literary Realism 1870-1910*, 1 (Fall 1967), 84-9.

Frohock, W. M. *Frank Norris.* Minneapolis: University of Minnesota Press, 1969.

Gaer, Joseph, ed. *Frank Norris: Bibliography and Biographical Data.* Berkeley: California Literary Research Project, Monograph No. 3, 1934.

Geismar, Maxwell. *Rebels and Ancestors: The American Novel, 1890-1915.* Boston: Houghton Mifflin and Company, 1953, 3-66.

Ginanni, Francis Ralph. "Impressionistic Techniques in the Novels of Frank Norris." Unpublished doctoral dissertation, Alburn University, 1970.

Goldsmith, Arnold L. "Charles and Frank Norris." *Western American Literature*, II (Spring 1967), 30-49.

Goldsmith, Arnold L. "The Development of Frank Norris's Philosophy." in *Studies in Honor of John Wilcox*, eds. A. Dayle Wallace and Woodburn O. Ross. Detroit: Wayne State University Press, 1958, 175-94.

Hart, James D., ed. *A Novelist in the Making*. Cambridge: Harvard University Press, 1970.

Hill, John S. *Checklist of Frank Norris*. Columbus: Charles E. Merrill Publishing, 1970.

Hoffmann, Charles G. "Norris and the Responsibility of the Novelist." *South Atlantic Quarterly*, LIV (October 1955), 508-15.

Johnson, George W. "Frank Norris and Romance." *American Literature*, XXXIII (March 1961), 52-63.

Johnson, George W. "The Frontier Behind Frank Norris' *McTeague*." *Huntington Library Quarterly*, XXVI (November 1962), 91-104.

Kaplan, Charles. "Norris's Use of Sources in *The Pit*." *American Literature*, XXV (March 1953), 75-84.

Kwiat, Joseph J. "Frank Norris: The Novelist as Social Critic and Literary Theorist." *Arizona Quarterly*, XVIII (Winter 1962), 319-28.

Lohf, Kenneth A., and Eugene P. Sheehy. *Frank Norris: A Bibliography*. Los Gatos, California: Talisman Press, 1959.

Lundy, Robert D. "The Making of *McTeague* and *The Octopus*." Unpublished doctoral dissertation, University of California, 1956.

Lynn, Kenneth S. *The Dream of Success*. Boston: Little, Brown, 1955, 158-207.

Marchand, Ernest. *Frank Norris: A Study*. Stanford: Stanford University Press, 1942.

Meyer, George W. "A New Interpretation of *The Octopus*." *College English*, IV (March 1943), 351-9.

Morgan, H. Wayne. *American Writers in Rebellion: From Mark Twain to Dreiser*. New York: Hill and Wang, 1965.

Pizer, Donald. "Another Look at *The Octopus*." *Nineteenth-Century Fiction*, X (December 1955), 217-24.

Pizer, Donald. "The Concept of Nature in Frank Norris' *The Octopus*." *American Quarterly*, XIV (Spring 1962), 73-80.

Pizer, Donald. "Evolutionary Ethical Dualism in Frank Norris' *Vandover and the Brute* and *McTeague*." *PMLA*,LXXVI (December 1961), 552-60.

Pizer, Donald. "Frank Norris' Definition of Naturalism." *Modern Fiction Studies*, VIII (Winter 1962-63), 408-10.

Pizer, Donald, ed. *The Literary Criticism of Frank Norris*. Austin: University of Texas Press, 1964.

Pizer, Donald. "The Masculine-Feminine Ethic in Frank Norris' Popular Novels." *Texas Studies in Language and Literature*, VI (Spring 1964), 84-91.

Pizer, Donald. "Nineteenth-Century American Naturalism: An Essay in Definition." *Bucknell Review*, XIII (December 1965), 1-18.

Pizer, Donald. *The Novels of Frank Norris.* Bloomington: Indiana University Press, 1966.

Pizer, Donald. "Synthetic Criticism and Frank Norris; Or, Mr. Marx, Mr. Taylor, and *The Octopus.*" *American Literature*, XXXIV (January 1963), 532-41.

Reninger, H. Williard. "Norris Explains *The Octopus:* A Correlation of His Theory and Practice." *American Literature*, XII (May 1940), 218-27.

Schneider, Robert W. *Five Novelists of the Progressive Era.* New York: Columbia University Press, 1965.

Schneider, Robert W. "Frank Norris: The Naturalist as Victorian." *Midcontinent American Studies Journal*, III (Spring 1962), 13-27.

Taylor, Walter Fuller. *The Economic Novel in America.* Chapel Hill; University of North Carolina Press, 1942, 282-306.

Vance, William L. "Romance in *The Octopus.*" *Genre*, III (June 1970), 111-36.

Walcutt, Charles Child. *American Literary Naturalism: A Divided Stream.* Minneapolis: University of Minnesota Press, 1956, 114-56.

Walcutt, Charles Child. "Frank Norris on Realism and Naturalism." *American Literature*, XIII (March 1941), 61-3.

Walcutt, Charles Child. "Frank Norris and the Search for Form." *University of Kansas City Review*, XIV (Winter 1947), 126-36.

Walker, Don D. "The Western Naturalism of Frank Norris." *Western American Literature*, II (Spring 1967), 14-29.

Walker, Franklin D., ed. *The Letters of Frank Norris.* San Francisco: The Book Club of California, 1956.

Walker, Franklin Dickerson. *Frank Norris: A Biography.* New York: Doubleday, Doran, 1932; reprinted, London: Russell & Russell, 1963.

EDGAR WILSON NYE
(Bill Nye)

Blair, Walter. "The Background of Bill Nye in American Humor." Unpublished doctoral dissertation, University of Chicago, 1931.

Chaplin, W. E. "Bill Nye." *Frontier*, XI (1931), 223-6.

Davidson, Levette J. "Bill Nye and *The Denver Tribune.*" *The Colorado Magazine*, IV (January 1928), 13-8.

Eitel, Edmund H. "Letters of Riley and Bill Nye." *Harpers Monthly Magazine*, CXXXVIII (1919), 473-84.

Larson, T. A., ed. *Bill Nye's Western Humor.* Lincoln, Nebraska: University of Nebraska Press, 1968.

Larson, T. A. "Laramie's Bill Nye." *1952 Brand Book.* Denver: Denver Westerners, 1953, 35-56.

Nye, Frank Wilson, ed. *Bill Nye: His Own Life.* New York: The Century Company, 1926.

Rush, Nixon Orwin, ed. *Letters of Edgar Wilson Nye.* Laramie: University of Wyoming Library, 1950.

Watson, Edgar. "Bill Nye's Experience." *Annals of Wyoming,* XVI (1944), 65-70.

SIGURD OLSON

Hertzel, Leo J. "What About Writers in the North?" *South Dakota Review,* V (Spring 1967), 3-19.

D. J. O'MALLEY

White, John I. " 'Kid' O'Malley: Montana's Cowboy Poet." *Montana Magazine of History,* XVII (July 1967), 60-73.

WILLIAM A. OWENS

Owens, William A. "Writing a Novel—Problem and Solution." *Southwest Review,* XL (Summer 1955), 254-61.

Pilkington, William T. *William A. Owens.* Southwest Writers Series, No. 17. Austin, Texas: Steck-Vaughn Company, 1968.

FRANCIS PARKMAN

Doughty, Howard. *Francis Parkman.* New York: Macmillan, 1962.

Feltskog, E. N., ed. *The Oregon Trail.* Madison: University of Wisconsin Press, 1969.

Hart, James D. "Patrician Among Savages: Francis Parkman's *The Oregon Trail.*" *Georgia Review,* X (Spring 1956), 69-73.

Jennings, F. P. "A Vanishing Indian: Francis Parkman versus His Sources." *Pennsylvania Magazine of History and Biography,* LXXXVII (July 1963), 306-23.

Lee, Robert Edson. *From West to East.* Urbana: University of Illinois Press, 1966, 69-81.

Levin, David. "Francis Parkman: *The Oregon Trail.*" in *Landmarks of American Writing,* ed. Hennig Cohen. New York: Basic Books, 1969, 79-89.

Levin, David. *History As Romantic Art.* Stanford: Stanford University Press, 1959.

Pease, Otis. *Parkman's History: The Historian as Literary Artist.* New Haven: Yale University Press, 1953.

Powers, William. "Bulkington as Henry Chatillon." *Western American Literature,* III (Summer 1968), 153-5.

Wade, Mason. *Francis Parkman: Heroic Historian.* New York: Viking, 1942.

Wade, Mason, ed. *The Journals of Francis Parkman.* 2 vols. New York: Harper, 1947.

Walsh, J. E. *"The California and Oregon Trail:* A Bibliographical Study." *New Colophon,* III (1950), 279-85.

KENNETH PATCHEN

Nelson, Raymond John. "An American Mysticism: The Example of Kenneth Patchen." Unpublished doctoral dissertation, Stanford University, 1969.

JAMES KIRKE PAULDING

Alderman, Ralph M. "James Kirke Paulding on Literature and the West." *American Literature,* XXVII (March 1955), 97-101.

GEORGE SESSIONS PERRY

Alexander, Stanley G. *George Sessions Perry.* Southwest Writers Series, No. 13. Austin, Texas: Steck-Vaughn Company, 1967.

Cowser, Robert C. "A Biographical and Critical Interpretation of George Sessions Perry." Unpublished doctoral dissertation, Texas Christian University, 1965.

Hairston, Maxine C. "The Development of George Sessions Perry as a Writer of Rural Texas." Unpublished doctoral dissertation, University of Texas, 1968.

JOHN PHOENIX
See George H. Derby

ALBERT PIKE

Allsopp, Frederick William. *Albert Pike: A Biography*. Little Rock, 1928.

Boyden, William L. *Bibliography of the Writings of Albert Pike: Prose, Poetry, Manuscript*. Washington, 1921.

Riley, Susan B. "The Life and Works of Albert Pike to 1860." Unpublished doctoral dissertation, George Peabody College, 1934.

Shrell, Darwin H. "Albert Pike (1809-1891). *"A Bibliographical Guide to the Study of Southern Literature*. Baton Rouge: Louisiana State University Press, 1969, 260-1.

KATHERINE ANNE PORTER

Allen, Charles A. "Southwestern Chronicle: Katherine Anne Porter." *Arizona Quarterly*, II (1946), 90-5.

Auchincloss, Louis. *Pioneers and Caretakers: A Study of American Women Novelists*. Minneapolis: University of Minnesota Press, 1965.

Baker, Howard. "The Upward Path: Notes on the Work of Katherine Anne Porter." *The Southern Review*, IV (January 1968), 1-19.

Becker, Laurence A. " 'The Jilting of Granny Weatherall': The Discovery of Pattern." *English Journal*, LV (December 1966), 1164-9.

Core, George. "Katherine Anne Porter (1894-   )." *A Bibliographical Guide to the Study of Southern Literature*. Baton Rouge: Louisiana State University Press, 1969, 268-72.

Emmons, Winfred S. *Katherine Anne Porter: The Regional Stories*. Southwest Writers Series, No. 6. Austin, Texas: Steck-Vaughn Company, 1967.

Hartley, Lodwick, and George Core, eds. *Katherine Anne Porter: A Critical Symposium*. Athens: University of Georgia Press, 1969.

Hendrick, George. *Katherine Anne Porter*. New York: Twayne, 1965.

Mooney, Harry John, Jr. *The Fiction and Criticism of Katherine Anne Porter*. Pittsburgh: University of Pittsburgh Press, 1957; revised edition, 1962.

Nance, William L. *Katherine Anne Porter and the Art of Rejection*. Chapel Hill: University of North Carolina Press, 1964.

Nance, William L. "Katherine Anne Porter and Mexico." *Southwest Review, LV (Spring 1970), 143-53*.

Partridge, Colin. " 'My Familiar Country': An Image of Mexico in the Work of Katherine Anne Porter." *Studies in Short Fiction*, VII (Fall 1970), 597-614.

Porter, Katherine Anne. *The Collected Essays and Occasional Writings of Katherine Anne Porter.* New York: Delacorte Press, 1970.

Schwartz, Edward. *Katherine Anne Porter: A Critical Bibliography.* New York: New York Public Library, 1953.

Smith, J. Oates. "Porter's *Noon Wine:* A Stifled Tragedy." *Renascence,* XVII (Spring 1965), 157-62.

Waldrip, Louise, and Shirley Ann Bauer. *A Bibiography of the Works of Katherine Anne Porter and a Bibliography of the Criticism of the Works of Katherine Anne Porter.* Metuchen, N.J.: Scarecrow Press, 1969.

Warren, Robert Penn. "Uncorrupted Consciousness: The Stories of Katherine Anne Porter." *Yale Review,* LV (Winter 1966), 280-90.

Welty, Eudora. "The Eye of the Story." *Yale Review,* LV (Winter 1966), 265-74.

West, Ray B., Jr. *Katherine Anne Porter.* Minneapolis: University of Minnesota Press, 1963.

West, Ray B., Jr. "Katherine Anne Porter and 'Historic Memory.' " *Hudson Review,* VI (Fall 1952), 16-27.

West, Ray B., Jr. "Katherine Anne Porter: Symbol and Theme in 'Flowering Judas.' " *Accent,* VII (Spring 1947), 182-7.

Wolfe, Peter. "The Problems of Granny Weatherall." *CLA Journal,* XI (December 1967), 142-8.

Young, Vernon A. "The Art of Katherine Anne Porter." *New Mexico Quarterly,* XV (Autumn 1945), 326-41.

WILLIAM SYDNEY PORTER
(O. Henry)

Clarkson, Paul S. *A Bibliography of William Sydney Porter.* Caldwell, Idaho: Caxton Printers, 1938.

Current-Garcia, Eugene. *O. Henry.* New York: Twayne Publishers, 1965.

Current-Garcia, Eugene. "William Sydney Porter ("O. Henry") (1962-1910)." *A Bibliographical Guide to the Study of Southern Literature.* Baton Rouge: Louisiana State University Press, 1969, 272-4.

Gallegly, J. S. "Background and Pattern of O. Henry's Texas Badman Stories." *Rice Institute Pamphlets,* XLII (October 1955), 1-32.

Gallegly, Joseph. *From Alamo Plaza to Jack Harris's Saloon; O. Henry and the Southwest He Knew.* The Hague: Mouton, 1971.

Langford, Gerald. *Alias O. Henry: A Biography of William Sydney Porter.* New York: The Macmillan Co., 1957.

Long, E. Hudson. "O. Henry (William Sydney Porter)." *American Literary Realism, 1870-1910* I (Fall 1967), 93-9.

Long, E. Hudson. *O. Henry: The Man and His Work.* New York: A. J. Barnes & Co., 1960.

Long, E. Hudson. "O. Henry as a Regional Artist." *Essays on American Literature in Honor of Jay B. Hubbell,* ed. Clarence Gohdes. Durham: Duke University Press, 1967, 229-40.

Payne, L. W., Jr. "The Humor of O. Henry." *Texas Review* IV (1918), 18-37.

Peel, Donald F. "A Critical Study of the Short Stories of O. Henry." *Northwest Missouri State College Studies,* XXV (November 1961), 3-24.

Robinson, Duncan, *et. al.* "O. Henry's Austin." *Southwest Review,* XXIV (July 1939), 388-410.

Rollins, Hyder E. "O. Henry's Texas." *Texas Review,* IV (1919), 295-307.

CHARLES PORTIS

Shuman, R. Baird. "Portis' *True Grit:* Adventure Story or *Entwicklungsroman?*" *English Journal,* XLIX (March 1970), 367-70.

J. F. POWERS

Hertzel, Leo J. "What About Writers in the North?" *South Dakota Review,* (Spring 1967), 3-19.

Stewart, D. H. "J. F. Powers' *Morte D'Urban as Western." Western American Literature,* V (Spring 1970), 31-44.

Wedge, G. F. "Two Bibliographies: Flannery O'Connor, J. F. Powers." *Critic,* II (Fall 1958), 59-70.

HERBERT QUICK

Keen, Carl L. "The Fictional Writings of Herbert Quick." Unpublished doctoral disseration, Michigan State University, 1968.

Morain, Frederick G. "Herbert Quick, Iowa Democrat." Unpublished doctoral disseration, Yale University, 1970.

WILLIAM MACLEOD RAINE

"Git Along, Ol' Typewriter." *Time*, (July 19, 1954), 82-4.

Loomis, C. Grant. "Folk Language in William McLeod Raine's West." *Tennessee Folklore Society Bulletin*, XXIV (December 1958), 131-48.

OPIE READ

Baird, Reed M. "The Works of Opie Read: A Study in Popular Culture." Unpublished doctoral dissertation, University of Michigan.

Linneman, William. "Opie Read and *The Arkansas-Traveler:* The Trials of a Regional Humor Magazine." *Midwest Folklore*, X Spring 1960), 5-10.

Rascoe, Burton. "Opie Read and Zane Grey." *Saturday Review of Literature*, XXI (November 11, 1939), 8.

MAYNE REID

Meyer, Roy W. "The Western Fiction of Mayne Reid." *Western American Literature*, III (Summer 1968), 115-32.

FREDERIC REMINGTON

Dykes, Jeff C. "Tentative Bibliographic Check Lists Western Illustrators: XXVI., Frederic Remington (1861-1909)." *American Book Collector*, XVI (November 1965), 20-31; (December 1965), 22-31; (January 1966), 26-31; (February 1966), 34-9; (March 1966), 21-7; (April 1966), 23-5.

McCracken, Harold. *Frederic Remington: Artist of the Old West.* Philadelphia: Lippincott, 1947.

McKown, Robin. *Painter of the Wild West: Frederic Remington.* New York: Messner, 1959.

Taft, Robert. *Artists and Illustrators of the Old West.* New York: Scribners, 1953.

White, G. Edward. *The Eastern Establishment and the Western Experience: The West of Frederic Remington, Theodore Roosevelt, and Owen Wister.* New Haven: Yale University Press, 1968.

KENNETH REXROTH

"An Interview with Kenneth Rexroth." *Critique*, X (Summer 1969), 313-31.

Foster, Richard. "The Voice of a Poet: Kenneth Rexroth." *Minnesota Review*, II (Spring 1962), 377-84.

Hartzell, James, and Richard Zumwinkle, comps. *Kenneth Rexroth: A Checklist of His Published Writings.* Los Angeles: Friends of the UCLA Library, 1967.

Lipton, Lawrence. "The Poetry of Kenneth Rexroth." *Poetry*, XC (June 1957), 168-80.

Rexroth, Kenneth. *The Alternative Society: Essays from the Other World.* New York: Herder and Herder, 1970.

Rexroth, Kenneth. *An Autobiographical Novel.* Garden City: Doubleday and Company, 1966.

Williams, W. C. "Two New Books by Kenneth Rexroth." *Poetry*, XC (June 1957), 180-90.

EUGENE MANLOVE RHODES

Compton, Adele O. "Eugene Manlove Rhodes: A Critical Study." Unpublished master's thesis, Eastern New Mexico University, 1966.

Day, Beth F. *Gene Rhodes, Cowboy.* New York: Julian Messner 1954.

Dearing, Frank V., ed. *The Best Novels and Stories of Eugene Manlove Rhodes.* Boston: Houghton Mifflin Company, *1949* See introductory remarks by J. Frank Dobie, xi-xxii.

DeVoto, Bernard. "The Novelists of the Cattle Country." *The Hired Man on Horseback*, by May Davidson Rhodes. Boston: Houghton Mifflin Company, 1938, xix-xiv.

Dobie, J. Frank. "Gene Rhodes: Cowboy Novelist." *Atlantic*, CLXXXIII (June 1949), 75-7.

Fife, Jim Lawrence. "Eugene Manlove Rhodes: Spokesman for Romantic Frontier Democracy." Unpublished doctoral dissertation, University of Iowa, 1965.

Fife, Jim L. "Two Views of the American West." *Western American Literature*, I(Spring 1966), 34-43.

Folsom, James K. "A Dedication to the Memory of Eugene Manlove Rhodes: 1869-1934." *Arizona and the West*, II (Winter 1969), 310-4.

Gaston, Edwin W., Jr. *Eugene Manlove Rhodes: Cowboy Chronicler.* Southwest Writers Series, No. 11. Austin, Texas: Steck-Vaughn Company, 1967.

Hoover, Edwin Hunt. "Eugene Manlove Rhodes Works Twenty Years on Novel." *Author & Journalist,* December, 1927.

Hutchinson, W. H. *A Bar Cross Liar. Bibliography of Eugene Manlove Rhodes Who Loved the West-That-Was When He Was Young,* Stillwater, Oklahoma: Redlands Press, 1959.

Hutchinson, W. H. *A Bar Cross Man: The Life and Personal Writings of Eugene Manlove Rhodes.* Norman: University of Oklahoma Press, 1956.

Hutchinson, W. H. "I Pay for What I Break." *Western American Literature,* I (Summer 1966), 91-6.

Hutchinson, W. H., ed. *The Rhodes Reader: Stories of Virgins, Villains, and Varmints.* Norman, Oklahoma: University of Oklahoma Press, 1957.

Hutchinson, W. H. "Virgins, Villains and Varmints." *Huntington Library Quarterly,* XVI (August 1953), 381-92.

Hutchinson, W. H. "The West of Eugene Manlove Rhodes." *Arizona and the West,* IX (Autumn 1967), 211-8.

Keleher, William A. *The Fabulous Frontier.* Santa Fe, 1946, 137-49.

Knibbs, Henry Herbert. "Gene Rhodes." *The Proud Sheriff.* Boston: Houghton Mifflin Company, 1935, iii-xxxviii.

Raine, William MacLeod. "Eugene Manlove Rhodes, American." *1945 Brand Book.* Denver, 1946, 47-58.

Rhodes, Mary Davison. *The Hired Man on Horseback: My Story of Eugene Manlove Rhodes.* Boston: Houghton Mifflin Company, 1938.

Rhodes, Mary Davison. "The Most Unforgettable Character I've Met." *Reader's Digest,* LXIV (January 1954), 21-6.

Ristvedt, Helen Smith. "Eugene Manlove Rhodes as Social Historian and Literary Artist." Unpublished master's thesis, Drake University, 1937.

Skillman, Richard, and Jerry C. Hoke. "The Portrait of the New Mexican in the Fiction of Eugene Rhodes." *Western Review* VI (Spring 1969), 26-36.

Work, Allene. "Eugene Manlove Rhodes: Chronicler of the Cow Country." Unpublished master's thesis, Southern Methodist University, 1948.

CONRAD RICHTER

Barnard, Kenneth J. "Presentation of the West in Conrad Richter's Trilogy." *Northern Ohio Quarterly,* XXIX (Autumn 1957), 224-34.

Barnes, Robert J. *Conrad Richter.* Southwest Writers Series, No. 14. Austin, Texas: Steck-Vaughn Company, 1968.

Carpenter, Frederic I. "Conrad Richter's Pioneers: Reality and Myth." *College English,* XII (November 1950), 77-83.

Edwards, Clifford D. *Conrad Richter's Ohio Trilogy: Its Ideas, Themes and Relationship to Literary Tradition.* The Hague: Mouton, 1971.

Flanagan, John T. "Conrad Richter: Romancer of the Southwest." *Southwest Review,* XLIII (Summer 1958), 189-96.

Flanagan, John T. "Folklore in the Novels of Conrad Richter." *Midwest Folklore,* II (Spring 1952), 5-14.

Gaston, Edwin W., Jr. *Conrad Richter.* New York: Twayne, 1965.

Kohler, Dayton. "Conrad Richter: Early Americana." *College English,* VIII (February 1947), 221-7.

LaHood, Marvin J. "Conrad Richter and Willa Cather: Some Similarities." *Xavier University Press,* IX (Spring 1970), 33-44.

LaHood, Marvin J. "*The Light in the Forest:* History as Fiction." *English Journal,* LV (March 1966), 298-304.

LaHood, Marvin J. "Richter's Early America." *The University Review,* XXX (June 1964), 311-6.

LaHood, Marvin J. "A Study of the Major Themes in the Work of Conrad Richter and His Place in the Tradition of the American Novel." Unpublished doctoral disseration, University of Notre Dame, 1962.

Pearce, T. M. "Conrad Richter." *New Mexico Quarterly,* XX (Autumn 1950), 371-3.

Richter, Conrad. "The Sea of Grass—A New Mexico Novel." *New Mexico Magazine,* XLIII (February 1965), 12-5.

Sutherland, Bruce. "Conrad Richter's Americana." *New Mexico Quarterly Review,* XV (Winter 1945), 413-22.

Young, David Lee. "The Art of Conrad Richter." Unpublished doctoral dissertation, Ohio State University, 1964.

LYNN RIGGS

Aughtry, Charles. "Lynn Riggs at the University of Oklahoma." *The Chronicles of Oklahoma,* XXXVII (Autumn 1959), 280-4.

Aughtry, Charles E. "Lynn Riggs, Dramatist: A Critical Biography." Unpublished doctoral dissertation, Brown University, 1959.

Benton, Joseph. "Some Personal Remembrances about Lynn Riggs." *The Chronicles of Oklahoma,* XXXIV (Autumn 1956), 296-301.

Erhard, Thomas A. *Lynn Riggs: Southwest Playwright.* Southwest Writers Series, No. 29. Austin, Texas: Steck-Vaughn Company, 1970.

Mitchell, Lee. "A Designer at Work." *Theatre Arts Monthly,* XVIII (November 1934), 874-7.

Wentz, John C. "American Regional Drama, 1920-40: Frustration and Fulfillment." *Modern Drama* VI (December 1963), 286-93.

Wilson, Eloise. "Lynn Riggs: Oklahoma Dramatist." Unpublished doctoral dissertation, University of Pennsylvania, 1957.

THEODORE ROETHKE

Burke, Kenneth. "The Vegetal Radicalism of Theodore Roethke." *Language as Symbolic Action*. Berkeley: The University of California Press, 1966, 254-81.

Dickey, James. "Theodore Roethke." *Poetry*, CV (November 1964), 120-4.

Everette, Oliver. "Theodore Roethke: The Poet as Teacher." *West Coast Review*, III (1968), 5-11.

Ferry, David. "Roethke's Poetry." *The Virginia Quarterly Review*, XLIII (Winter 1967), 169-73.

Heilman, Robert. "Theodore Roethke: Personal Notes." *Shenandoah*, XVI (Autumn 1964), 55-64.

Heron, Philip E. "The Vision of Meaning: Theodore Roethke's Frau Bauman, Frau Schmidt, and Frau Schwartze." *Western Speech*, XXXIV (Winter 1970), 29-33.

Heyen, William. "The Divine Abyss: Theodore Roethke's Mysticism." *Texas Studies in Literature and Language*, XI (Winter 1969), 1051-68.

Hollenberg, S. W. "Theodore Roethke: Bibliography." *Twentieth-Century Literature*, XII (January 1967), 216-21.

Kramer, Hilton. "The Poetry of Theodore Roethke." *Western Review*, XVIII (Winter 1954), 131-46.

Kunitz, Stanley. "Roethke: Poet of Transformations." *The New Republic*, CLII (January 23, 1965), 23-9.

Labell, Jenijoy. "Theodore Roethke and Tradition." Unpublished doctoral dissertation, University of California, San Diego, 1969.

Lee, Charlotte I. "The Line as a Rhythmic Unit in the Poetry of Theodore Roethke." *Speech Monographs*, XXX (March 1963), 15-22.

McLeod, James R. *Theodore Roethke: A Manuscript Checklist*. Kent, Ohio: Kent State University Press, 1971.

McMichael, James. "The Poetry of Theodore Roethke." *The Southern Review*, V (Winter 1969), 4-25.

Malkoff, Karl. "Cleansing the Doors of Perception." *Minnesota Review*, V (October-December 1965), 342-8.

Malkoff, Karl. *Theodore Roethke: An Introduction to the Poetry*. New York: Columbia University Press, 1966.

Matheson, John William. "Theodore Roethke: A Bibliography." Unpublished master's thesis, University of Washington School of Librarianship, 1958.

Mazzaro, Jerome. "Theodore Roethke and the Failure of Language." *Modern Poetry Studies*, I (July 1970), 73-96.

Meredith, William. "A Steady Storm of Correspondence: Theodore Roethke's Long Journey Out of the Self." *Shenandoah*, XVI (Autumn 1964), 41-54.

Mills, Ralph J., Jr. "Roethke's Garden." *Poetry*, C (April 1962), 54-9.

Mills, Ralph J., Jr. "Theodore Roethke: The Lyric of the Self." in Edward Hungerford, ed. *Poets in Progress: Critical Prefaces to Ten Contemporary Americans*. Evanston: Northwestern University Press, 1962, 3-23.

Mills, Ralph J., Jr. *Theodore Roethke*. Minneapolis: University of Minnesota, 1963.

Northwest Review, XI (Summer 1971), 1-159.

Roethke, Theodore. *On the Poet and His Craft: Selected Prose of Theodore Roethke*, ed. Ralph Mills, Jr. Seattle: University of Washington Press, 1965.

Schumacker, Paul J. "The Unity of Being: A Study of Theodore Roethke's Poetry." *The Ohio University Review*, XII (1970), 20-40.

Schwartz, Delmore. "The Cunning and the Craft of the Unconscious and the Preconscious." *Poetry*, XCIV (June 1959), 203-5.

Seager, Allan. *The Glass House: The Life of Theodore Roethke*. New York: McGraw-Hill Book Company, 1968.

Seager, Allan, *et. al.* "An Evening with Ted Roethke." *Michigan Quarterly Review*, VI (Fall 1967), 227-45.

Seymour-Smith, Martin. "Where Is Mr. Roethke?" *Black Mountain Review*, I (Spring 1954), 40-7.

Southworth, James G. "The Poetry of Theodore Roethke." *College English*, XXI (March 1960), 326-30, 335-8.

Staples, Hugh. "The Rose in the Sea-Wind: A Reading of Theodore Roethke's North American Sequence." *American Literature*, XXXVI (May 1964), 189-203.

Stein, Arnold, ed. *Theodore Roethke: Essays on the Poetry*. Seattle: University of Washington Press, 1965.

Wain, John. "Theodore Roethke." *Critical Quarterly*, VI (Winter 1964), 322-38.

Winters, Yvor. "The Poems of Theodore Roethke." *Kenyon Review*, III (Autumn 1941), 514-6.

WILL ROGERS

Alworth, E. Paul. "The Humor of Will Rogers." Unpublished doctoral dissertation, University of Missouri, 1958.

Day, Donald. *Will Rogers, A Biography.* New York, 1962.

Eitner, Walter H. "Will Rogers: Another Look At His Act." *Kansas Quarterly,* II (Spring 1970), 46-52.

Rogers, Will. *The Autobiography of Will Rogers,* ed. Donald Day. Boston: Houghton Mifflin Company, 1949.

OLE ROLVAAG

Baker, Joseph E. "Western Man Against Nature: *Giants in the Earth.*" *College English,* IV (October 1942), 19-26.

Bjork, Kenneth O. "The Unknown Rölvaag: Secretary in the Norwegian-American Historical Association." *Norwegian-American Stud. and Rec.,* XI (1940), 114-49.

Boynton, Percy H. "O. E. Rölvaag and the Conquest of the Pioneer." *English Journal,* XVIII (September 1929), 535-42.

Boynton, Percy H. "Ole Edvart Rölvaag." *America in Contemporary Fiction.* Chicago: University of Chicago Press, 1927, 225-40.

Fox, Maynard. "The Bearded Face Set Toward the Sun." *Ball State Teacher's College Forum,* I (Winter 1960-61), 62-4.

Gvåle, Gudrun Hovde. *Ole Edvart Rölvaag: Nordmann og Amerikanar.* Oslo: Aschehoug, 1962.

Heitmann, John "Ole Edvart Rolvaag." *Norwegian-American Stud. and Rec.,* XII (1941), 144-66.

Huagen, Einar. "O. E. Rölvaag: Norwegian-American." *Norwegian-American Stud. and Rec.,* VII (1933), 53-73.

Jorgenson, Theodore. "The Main Factors in Rölvaag's Authorship." *Norwegian-American Stud. and Rec.,* X (1938), 135-51.

Jorgenson, Theodore and Nora O. Solum. *Ole Edvart Rölvaag: A Biography.* New York: Harper and Brothers, 1939.

Nelson, Pearl. "Rölvaag." *Prairie Schooner,* III (Spring 1929), 156-9.

Olson, Julius E. "Rölvaag's Novels of Norwegian Pioneer Life in the Dakotas." *Scandinavian Studies and Notes,* IX (1927), 45-55.

Parrington, Vernon. "Ole Rölvaag's 'Giants in the Earth.'" *The Beginnings of Critical Realism in American: 1860-1920.* New York: Harcourt, Brace and World, Inc., 1930, 387-96.

Reigstad, Paul M. "The Art and Mind of O. E. Rölvaag." Unpublished doctoral disseration, University of New Mexico, 1958.

Solum, Nora O. "The Sources of the Rölvaag Biography." *Norwegian-American Stud. and Rec.,* XI (1940), 150-9.

Steensma, Robert. "Rölvaag and Turner's Frontier Thesis." *North Dakota Quarterly*, XXVII (Autumn 1959), 100-4.

Stevens, Robert Lowell. "Ole Edvart Rölvaag: A Critical Study of His Norwegian-American Novels." *Dissertation Abstracts*, XVI (May 1956), 966-7.

White, George Leroy. "O. E. Rolvaag—Prophet of a People." *Scandinavian Themes in American Fiction.* Philadelphia, 1937, 97-108.

THEODORE ROOSEVELT

Barsness, John A. "Theodore Roosevelt as Cowboy: The Virginian as Jacksonian Man." *American Quarterly*, XXI (Fall 1969), 609-19.

Dornbusch, Clyde H. "Theodore Roosevelt's Literary Taste and Relationships with Authors." Unpublished doctoral dissertation, Duke University, 1957.

Fenton, Charles. "Theodore Roosevelt as a Man of Letters." *Western Humanities Review*, XIII (August 1959), 369-74.

Lewis, Merrill E. "American Frontier History as Literature: Studies in Historiography of George Bancroft, Frederick Jackson Turner, and Thoeodore Roosevelt." Unpublished doctoral disseration, University of Utah, 1968.

Moers, Ellen. "Teddy Roosevelt: Literary Feller." Columbia University Forum, VI (Summer 1963), 10-6.

Walker, Don D. "Wister, Roosevelt and James: A Note on the Western." *American Quarterly*, XII (Fall 1960), 358-66.

White, G. Edward. *The Eastern Establishment and the Western Experience: The West of Frederic Remington, Theodore Roosevelt, and Owen Wister.* New Haven: Yale University Press, 1968.

CHARLES M. RUSSELL

Adams, Ramon F., and Homer E. Fitzman. *Charles M. Russell, The Cowboy Artist.* Pasadena: Trail's End Publishing Co., 1948.

Brunvand, Jan Harold. "From Western Folklore to Fiction in the Stories of Charles M. Russell." Western Review, V (Summer 1968), 41-9.

Ellsberg, William. "Charles, Thou Art a Rare Blade." *American West*, VI (March 1969), 4-9; (May 1969), 40-3, 62.

GEORGE F. RUXTON

Gatson, Edwin W., Jr. *The Early Novel of the Southwest.* Albuquerque: University of New Mexico Press, 1961.

Hafen, LeRoy, and others, ed. *Ruxton of the Rockies.* Norman: University of Oklahoma Press, 1950.

Sutherland, Bruce. "George Frederick Ruxton in North America." *Southwest Review,* XXX (Autumn 1944), 86-91.

MARI SANDOZ

Lowe, David. "A Meeting with Mari Sandoz.'" *Prairie Schooner,* XLII (Spring 1968), 21-6.

"Mari Sandoz: 1935." *Prairie Schooner,* XLI (Summer 1967), 172-7.

Nicoll, Bruce H. "Mari Sandoz: Nebraska Loner." *The American West,* II (Spring 1965), 32-6.

Posner, David. "A Meeting with Mari Sandoz." *Prairie Schooner,* XLII (Spring 1968), 21-6.

Switzer, Dorothy Nott. "Mari Sandoz's Lincoln Years." *Prairie Schooner,* XLV (Summer 1971), 107-15.

ROSS SANTEE

Dykes, Jeff C. "Tentative Bibliographic Check Lists of Western Illustrators: XXVIII, Ross Santee (1888-1965)." American Book Collector, XVI (Summer 1966), 23-8.

Ford, Moselle A. "Ross Santee: Author and Artist of the Southwest." Unpublished master's thesis, Texas Western College, 1966.

Houston, Neal B. *Ross Santee.* Southwest Writers Series, No. 18. Austin, Texas: Steck-Vaughn Company, 1968.

WILLIAM SAROYAN

Burgum, Edwin B. "The Lonesome Young Man on the Flying Trapeze." *Virginia Quarterly Review,* XX (Summer 1944), 392-403.

Carpenter, Frederic I. "The Time of Saroyan's Life." *Pacific Spectator,* I (Winter 1947), 88-96.

Fisher, William J. "What Ever Happened to Saroyan?" *College English,* XVI (March 1955), 336-40.

Floan, Howard R. *William Saroyan.* New York: Twayne, 1966.

Hatcher, Harlan. "William Saroyan." *English Journal,* XXVIII (March 1939), 169-77.

Kherdian, David. *A Bibliography of William Saroyan, 1934-1964.* San Francisco: Roger Beacham, 1965.

Krickel, Edward. "Cozzens and Saroyan: A Look at Two Reputations." *Georgia Review, XXIV (Fall 1970), 281-96.*

LaCroix, Paul-Henri. "William Saroyan and the Short Story." Unpublished master's thesis, University of Montreal, 1959.

Morris, David W. "A Critical Analysis of William Saroyan." Unpublished doctoral dissertation, Denver University, 1960.

Nathan, George Jean. "Saroyan: Whirling Dervish of Fresno." *American Mercury,* II (November 1940), 303-8.

Remenyi, Joseph. "William Saroyan: A Portrait." *College English,* VI (November 1944), 92-100.

Rahv, Philip. "William Saroyan: A Minority Report." *American Mercury,* LVII (September 1943), 371-7.

Remenyi, Joseph. "William Saroyan: A Portrait." *College English,* VI (November 1944), 92-100.

Schulberg, Budd. "Saroyan: Ease and Unease on the Flying Trapeze." *Esquire,* LIV (October 1960), 85-91.

Singer, Felix. "Saroyan at 57: The Daring Young Man After the Fall." Trace, XV (Spring 1966), 2-5.

Wilson, Edmund. "The Boys in the Back Room." *A Literary Chronicle: 1920-1950.* Garden City, New York: Doubleday and Company, 1956, 222-7.

DOROTHY SCARBOROUGH

Beard, Joyce J. "Dorothy Scarborough: Texas Regionalist." Unpublished master's thesis, Texas Christian University, 1965.

Heavens, Jean. "Dorothy Scarborough—Fictional Historian." Unpublished master's thesis, University of Texas at El Paso, 1968.

JACK SCHAEFFER

Dieter, Lynn. "Behavioral Objectives in the English Classroom: A Model." *English Journal,* LIX (December 1970), 1258-62, 1271.

Haslam, G. W. "Jack Schaefer's Frontier: The West as Human Testing Ground." *Rocky Mountain Review,* IV (1967), 59-71.

Johnson, Dorothy M. "Jack Schaefer's People." Introduction to *The Short Novels of Jack Schaefer*. Boston: Houghton Mifflin Company, 1967.

Mikkelsen, Robert. "The Western Writer: Jack Schaefer's Use of the Western Frontier." *Western Humanities Review*, VIII (Spring 1954), 151-5.

MARK SCHORER

Bluefarb, Sam. "What We Don't Know *Can* Hurt Us." *Studies in Short Fiction*, V (Spring 1968), 269-74.

ROBERT W. SERVICE

Bucco, Martin. "Folk Poetry of Robert W. Service." *Alaska Review*, Il (Fall 1965), 16-26.

LUKE SHORT
(Frederick Glidden)

Nye, Russel B. *The Unembarrassed Muse: The Popular Arts in America*. New York: The Dial Press, 1970.

Short, Luke. "Ernest Haycox: An Appreciation." *The Call Number*, XXV (Fall 1963-Spring 1964), 2-3.

BERTHA SINCLAIR
See B. M. Bower

UPTON SINCLAIR

Becker, George J. "Upton Sinclair: Quixote in a Flivver." *College English*, XXI (December 1959), 133-40.

Blumenthal, W. A. "Prolific: Writer's Cramp versus Literary Fecundity." *American Book Collector*, VIII (May 1958), 3-10.

Brooks, Van Wyck. "The Novels of Upton Sinclair." *Emerson and Others*. New York: E. P. Dutton, 1958, 209-17.

Gottesman, Ronald. "Upton Sinclair: An Annotated Bibliographical Catalogue, 1894-1932." Unpublished doctoral dissertation, University of Indiana, 1964.

Hicks, Granville. "The Survival of Upton Sinclair." *College English*, IV (January 1943), 213-20.

Soderbergh, Peter A. "Upton Sinclair and Hollywood." *Midwest Quarterly*, XI (January 1970), 173-91.

CHARLES A. SIRINGO

Adams, Clarence Siringo. "Fair Trial at Encinoso." *True West*, V (March-April 1966), 32 ff.

Clark, Neil M. "Close Calls: An Interview with Charles A. Siringo." *The American Magazine*, CVII (January 1929), 38 ff.

Hammond, John Hays. "Strong Men of the West." *Scribner's Magazine*, LXXVII (February, March 1925), 115-25, 246-56.

Nolen, O. W. "Charley Siringo." *Cattleman*, XXXVIII (December 1951), 50 ff.

Peavy, Charles D. *Charles A. Siringo: A Texas Picaro*. Southwest Writers Series, No. 3. Austin, Texas: Steck-Vaughn Company, 1967.

Thorp, Raymond W. "Cowboy Charley Siringo." *True West*, XII (January-February 1965), 32 ff.

GARY SNYDER

Altieri, Charles. "Gary Snyder's Lyric Poetry: Dialectic as Ecology." *Far Point*, IV (Spring-Summer 1970), 55-65.

Benoit, Raymond. "The New American Poetry." *Thought*, XLIV (Summer 1969), 201-18.

Howard, Richard. *Alone with America: Essays on the Art of Poetry in the United States*. New York: Atheneum, 1969, 485-98.

Lyon, Thomas J. "The Ecological Vision of Gary Snyder." *Kansas Quarterly*, I (Spring 1970), 117-24.

Lyon, Thomas J. "Gary Snyder, a Western Poet." *Western American Literature*, III (Fall 1968), 207-16.

Parkinson, Thomas. "The Poetry of Gary Snyder." *Southern Review*, IV (Summer 1968), 616-32.

VIRGINIA SORENSEN

Bradford, Mary L. "Virginia Sorensen: A Saving Remnant." *Dialogue: A Journal of Mormon Thought,* IV (Autumn 1969), 56-64.

JEAN STAFFORD

Burns, Stuart L. "Counterpoint in Jean Stafford's *The Mountain Lion." Critique,* IX (1967), 20-32.

Hassan, Ihab H. "Jean Stafford: The Expense of Style and the Scope of Sensibility." *Western Review,* XIX (Spring 1955), 185-203.

WILLIAM STAFFORD

Benoit, Raymond. "The New American Poetry." *Thought,* XLIV (Summer 1969), 201-18.

"A Conversation between William Stafford and Primus St. John." *Voyages,* III (Spring 1970), 70-9.

Gerber, Philip L., and Robert J. Gemmett, eds. "Keeping the Lines Wet: A Conversation with William Stafford." *Prairie Schooner,* XLIV (Summer 1970), 123-36.

Greiner, Charles F. "Stafford's 'Traveling Through the Dark': A Discussion of Style." *English Journal,* LV (November 1966), 1015-8.

Howard, Richard. *Alone with America: Essays on the Art of Poetry in the United States.* New York: Atheneum, 1969, 499-506.

Hugo, Richard. "Problems with Landscapes in Early Stafford Poems." *Kansas Quarterly,* II (Spring 1970), 33-8.

Kelley, Partick. "Legend and Ritual." *Kansas Quarterly,* II (Spring 1970), 28-31.

McMillan, Sammuel H. "On William Stafford and His Poems: A Selected Bibliography." *Tennessee Poetry Journal,* II (Spring 1969), 21-2.

Miller, Tom P. " 'In Dear Detail, by Ideal Light': The Poetry of William Stafford." *Southwest Review,* LVI (Autumn 1971), 341-5.

Moran, Ronald, and George Lensing. "The Emotive Imagination: A New Departure in American Poetry." *Southern Review,* III (January 1967), 51-67.

Ramsey, Paul. "What the Light Struck." *Tennessee Poetry Journal,* II (Spring 1969), 17-20.

Roberts, J. Russell, Sr. "Listening to the Wilderness with William Stafford." *Western American Literature*, III (Fall 1968), 217-26.
Sumner, D. Nathan. "The Poetry of William Stafford." *Research Studies*, XXXVI (September 1968), 187-95.

WALLACE STEGNER

Eisinger, Chester E. *Fiction of the Forties*. Chicago: University of Chicago Press, 1963, 324-8.
Eisinger, Chester E. "Twenty Years of Wallace Stegner." *College English*, XX (December 1958), 110-6.
Flora, Joseph M. "Vardis Fisher and Wallace Stegner: Teacher and Student." *Western American Literature*, V (Summer 1970), 122-8.
Hairston, Joe B. "Wallace Stegner." Unpublished master's thesis, University of Texas, 1966.
Hudson, Lois Phillips. "The Big Rock Candy Mountain: No Roots— and No Frontier." *South Dakota Review*, IX (Spring 1971), 3-13.
Milton, John. "Conversation with Wallace Stegner." *South Dakota Review*, X (Spring 1971), 45-57.
Tyler, Robert L. "The I.W.W. and the West." *American Quarterly*, XII (Summer 1960), 175-87.

JOHN STEINBECK

Alexander, Stanley. "Cannery Row: Steinbeck's Pastoral Poem." *Western American Literature*, II (Winter 1968), 281-95.
Alexander, Stanley. "The Conflict of Form in *Tortilla Flat*." *American Literature*, XL (March 1968), 58-66.
Alexander, Stanley Gerald. "Primitivism and Pastoral Form in John Steinbeck's Early Fiction." Unpublished doctoral dissertation, University of Texas, 1965.
Antico, John. "A Reading of Steinbeck's 'Flight.' " *Modern Fiction Studies*, XI (Spring 1965), 45-53.
Astro, Richard. "Into the Cornucopia: Steinbeck's Vision of Nature and the Ideal Man." Unpublished doctoral dissertation, University of Washington, 1969.
Astro, Richard. "Steinbeck and Ricketts: Escape or Commitment in *The Sea of Cortez*." *Western American Literature*, VI (Summer 1971), 109-21.
Astro, Richard. "Steinbeck's Post-War Trilogy: A Return to Nature and Natural Man." *Twentieth Century Literature*, XVI (April 1970), 109-22.

Astro, Richard, and Tetsumaro Hayaskhi. *Steinbeck: The Man and His Work.* Corvallis: Oregon State University Press, 1971.

Beebe, Maurice, and Jackson R. Bryer. "Criticism of John Steinbeck: A Selected Checklist." *Modern Fiction Studies,* XI (Spring 1965), 90-103.

Bleeker, Gary Wallace. "Setting and Animal Tropes in the Fiction of John Steinbeck." Unpublished doctoral dissertation, University of Nebraska, 1969.

Bowron, Bernard. *"The Grapes of Wrath:* A 'Wagons West' Romance." *Colorado Quarterly,* III (Summer 1954), 84-91.

Bracher, Frederick. "Steinbeck and the Biological View of Man." *Pacific Spectator,* II (1948), 14-29.

Brown, D. Russell. "The Natural Man in John Steinbeck's Non-Teleological Tales." *Ball State University Forum,* VII (Spring 1966), 47-52.

Casimar, Louis J. "Human Emotion and the Early Novels of John Steinbeck." Unpublished doctoral dissertation, University of Texas, 1966.

Chametzky, Jules. "The Ambivalent Endings of *The Grapes of Wrath." Modern Fiction Studies,* XI (Spring 1965), 34-44.

Champney, Freeman. "John Steinbeck, Californian." *Antioch Review,* VII (1947), 345-62.

Ditsky, John M. "Music from a Dark Cave: Organic Form in Steinbeck's Fiction." *The Journal of Narrative Technique,* I (January 1971), 59-67.

Fontenrose, Joseph. *John Steinbeck: An Introduction and Interpretation.* New York: Barnes and Noble, 1963.

French, Warren. *A Companion to The Grapes of Wrath.* New York, 1963.

French, Warren G. "Another Look at *The Grapes of Wrath." Colorado Quarterly,* III (Winter 1955), 337-43.

French, Warren. *John Steinbeck.* New York: Twayne, 1961.

French, Warren. "John Steinbeck." *Fifteen Modern American Authors,* edited by Jackson R. Bryer. Durham: Duke University Press, 1969, 369-87.

Galbraith, John Kenneth. "John Steinbeck: Footnote for a Memoir." *Atlantic,* CCXXIV (November 1969), 65-7.

Goldhurst, William. *"Of Mice and Men*: John Steinbeck's Parable of the Curse of Cain." *Western American Literature,* VI (Summer 1971), 123-35.

Goldsmith, Arnold L. "Thematic Rhythm in *The Red Pony." College English,* XXVI (February 1965), 391-4.

Golemba, Henry L. "Steinbeck's Attempt to Escape the Literary Fallacy." *Modern Fiction Studies,* XV (Summer 1969), 231-9.

Gordon, Walter K. "Steinbeck's 'Flight': Journey *to* or *from* Maturity?" *Studies in Short Fiction,* III (Summer 1966), 453-5.

Griffin, R. J., and W. A. Freedman. "Machines and Animals: Pervasive Motifs in *The Grapes of Wrath." Journal of English and Germanic Philology,* LXII (July 1963), 569-80.

Grommon, A. H. "Who Is 'The Leader of the People'?" English Journal, XLVIII (November 1959), 449-61.

Hayashi, Tetsumaro. "John Steinbeck: A Checklist of Unpublished Ph.D. Dissertations (1946-1967)." *Serif,* V (December 1968), 30-1.

Hayashi, Tetsumaro. *John Steinbeck: A Concise Bibliography, (1930-1965).* Metuchen, N.J.: The Scarecrow Press, Inc., 1967.

Hayashi, Tetsumaro, ed. *Steinbeck Quarterly,* I (1968—). Ball State University, Muncie, Indiana.

Hilton, William C. "John Steinbeck: An Annotated Bibliography of Criticism, 1936-1963." Unpublished master's thesis, Wayne State University, 1965.

Houghton, Donald E. " 'Westering' in 'Leader of the People.' " *Western American Literature,* IV (Summer 1969), 117-24.

Johnson, Curtis L. "Steinbeck: A Suggestion for Research." *Modern Fiction Studies,* XI (Spring 1965), 75-8.

Jones, Lawrence William. " 'A Little Play in Your Head': Parable Form in John Steinbeck's Post-War Fiction." *Genre,* III (March 1970), 55-63.

Justus, James H. "The Transient World of *Tortilla Flat." Western Review,* VII (Spring 1970), 55-60.

Karsten, Ernest E., Jr. "Thematic Structure in *The Pearl. " English Journal,* LIV (January 1965), 1-7.

Kinney, Arthur F. "The Arthurian Cycle in *Tortilla Flat." Modern Fiction Studies,* XI (Spring 1965), 11-20.

Levant, Howard. *"Tortilla Flat:* The Shape of John Steinbeck's Career." *PMLA,* LXXXV (October 1970), 1087-95.

Levant, Howard. "The Unity of *In Dubious Battle:* Violence and Dehumanization." *Modern Fiction Studies,* XL (Spring 1965), 21-33.

Lisca, Peter. "John Steinbeck: A Literary Biography." *Steinbeck and His Critics: A Record of Twenty-five Years,* eds. E. W. Tedlock, Jr., and C. V. Wicker. Albuquerque: University of New Mexico Press, 1957, 3-22.

Lisca, Peter. "Steinbeck and Hemingway: Suggestions for a Comparative Study." *Steinbeck Newsletter,* II (Spring 1969), 9-17.

Lisca, Peter. "Steinbeck's Image of Man and His Decline as a Writer." *Modern Fiction Studies,* XI (Spring 1965), 3-10.

Lisca, Peter. *The Wide World of John Steinbeck.* New Brunswick: Rutgers University Press, 1958.

Lisca, Peter, *et. al.* "John Steinbeck Special Number." *Modern Fiction Studies*, XI (Spring 1965), 3-103.

McMahan, Elizabeth E. " 'The Chrysanthemums': Study of a Woman's Sexuality." *Modern Fiction Studies*, XIV (Winter 1968-69), 453-8.

McWilliams, Carey. "A Man, A Place, and a Time." *The American West*, VII (May 1970), 4-8, 38-40, 62-4.

Marcus, Mordecai. "The Lost Dream of Sex and Childbirth in 'The Chrysanthemums.' " *Modern Fiction Studies*, XI (Spring 1965), 54-8.

Marks, Lester Jay. *Thematic Design in the Novels of John Steinbeck.* The Hague: Mouton, 1970.

Metzger, C. R. "Steinbeck's Version of the Pastoral." *Modern Fiction Studies*, VI (Summer 1960), 115-24.

Moore, Harry Thornton. *The Novels of John Steinbeck: A First Critical Study.* Chicago: Normandie House, 1939.

Morsberger, Robert E. "In Defense of 'Westering.' " *Western American Literature*, V (Summer 1970), 143-6.

Nelson, H. S. "Steinbeck's Politics Then and Now." *Antioch Review*, XXVII (Spring 1967), 118-33.

Nimitz, Jack. "Ecology in *The Grapes of Wrath." Hartford Studies in Literature*, II (No. 2), 165-8.

Nossen, Evon. "The Beast-Man Theme in the Work of John Steinbeck." *Ball State University Forum*, VII (Spring 1966), 52-64.

O'Connor, Richard. *John Steinbeck.* American Writers Series. New York: McGraw-Hill, 1970.

Powell, Lawrence Clark. "Toward a Bibliography of John Steinbeck." *The Colophon*, New Series, III (Autumn 1938), 558-68.

Pratt, John Clark. *John Steinbeck.* Contemporary Writers in Christian Perspective. Grand Rapids: William B. Eerdmans, 1970.

Ross, Woodburn O. "John Steinbeck: Naturalism's Priest." *College English*, X (1949), 432-7.

Rundell, Walter Jr. "Steinbeck's Image of the West." *The American West*, I (Spring 1964), 4-17, 79.

Scoville, Samuel. "The *Weltanschauung* of Steinbeck and Hemingway: An Analysis of Themes." *English Journal*, LVI (January 1967), 60-3, 66.

Shockley, Martin. "Christian Symbolism in *The Grapes of Wrath." College English*, XVIII (November 1956), 87-90.

Shuman, R. Baird. "Initiation Rites in Steinbeck's *The Red Pony." English Journal*, LIX (December 1970), 1252-5.

Slade, Leonard A., Jr. "The Use of Biblical Allusions in *The Grapes of Wrath."CLA Journal*, XI (March 1968), 241-7.

Steele, Joan. "John Steinbeck: A Checklist of Biographical, Critical, and Bibliographical Material." *Bulletin of Bibliography*, XXIV (May-August 1965), 149-152, 162-3.

Taylor, Horace P., Jr. "John Steinbeck: The Quest." *McNeese Review*, XVI (1965), 33-45.

Tedlock, E. W., Jr., and C. V. Wicker, editors. *Steinbeck and His Critics: A Record of Twenty-Five Years*. Albuquerque: University of New Mexico Press, 1957.

Tuttleton, James W. "Steinbeck in Russia: The Rhetoric of Praise and Blame." *Modern Fiction Studies*, XI (Spring 1965), 79-89.

Wallis, Prentiss Bascom. "John Steinbeck: The Symbolic Family." Unpublished doctoral dissertation, University of Kansas, 1966.

Watt, F. G. *John Steinbeck*. New York: Grove Press: Edinburgh: Oliver and Boyd, 1962.

West, Philip J. "Steinbeck's 'The Leader of the People': A Crisis in Style." *Western American Literature*, V (Summer 1970), 137-41.

Woodress, James. "John Steinbeck: Hostage to Fortune." *South Atlantic Quarterly*, LXIII (Summer 1964), 385-97.

Wyatt, Bryant N. "Experimentation as Technique: The Protest Novels of John Steinbeck." *Discourse*, XII (Spring 1969), 143-53.

GEORGE STERLING

Coblentz, S. A. "George Sterling: Western Phenomenon." *Arizona Quarterly*, XIII (Spring 1957), 54-60.

Cross, Dalton, ed. "Seventeen George Sterling Letters." *Jack London Newsletter*, I (July-December 1968), 41-61.

Dunbar, John R. "Letters of George Sterling to Carey McWilliams." *California Historical Society Quarterly*, XLVI (1967), 235-52.

Johnson, Cecil, ed. *A Bibliography of the Writing of George Sterling*. Folcroft, Pennsylvania: Folcroft Press, Inc., 1969.

JAMES STEVENS

Clare, Warren L. "Big Jim Stevens: A Study in Pacific Northwest Literature." Unpublished doctoral dissertation, Washington State University, 1967.

Clare, Warren L. "James Stevens: The Laborer and Literature." *Research Studies*, IV (December 1964), 355-67.

ROBERT LOUIS STEVENSON

Issler, Anne Roller. "Robert Louis Stevenson in Monterey." *Pacific Historical Review*, XXXIV (August 1965), 305-21.

MICHAEL STRAIGHT

Milton, John R. *Three West: Conversations with Vardis Fisher, Max Evans, Michael Straight.* Vermillion, South Dakota: Dakota Press, 1970.

IDAH MEACHAM STROBRIDGE

Amaral, Anthony. "Idah Meacham Strobridge: First Woman of Nevada Letters." *Nevada Historical Society Quarterly*, X (Fall 1967), 5-12.

RUTH SUCKOW

Baker, Joseph E. "Regionalism in the Middle West." *American Review*, V (March 1935), 603-14.

Frederick, John T. "Ruth Suckow and the Middle Western Literary Movement." *English Journal*, XX (January 1931), 1-8.

Kissane, Leedice McAnelly. *Ruth Suckow.* New York: Twayne Publisher, 1969.

Mohr, Martin. "Ruth Suckow: Regionalism and Beyond." Unpublished master's thesis, University of Iowa, 1955.

Mott, Frank Luther. "Ruth Suckow." *A Book of Iowa Authors*, ed. Johnson Brigham. Des Moines, 1930, 215-24.

Nuhn, Ferner, ed. "Cycle of the Seasons in Iowa: Unpublished Diary of Ruth Suckow." *The Iowan*, IX (October-November 1960; December-January 1960-61; April-May 1961).

Paluka, Frank. "Ruth Suckow: A Calender of Letters." *Books at Iowa.* [University of Iowa Library] (October 1964-April 1965).

Stewart, Margaret O'Brien. "A Critical Study of Ruth Suckow's Fiction." Unpublished doctoral dissertation, University of Illinois, 1960.

ALAN SWALLOW

Harris, Mark. "Obituary Three for Alan Swallow." *Modern Fiction Studies,* XV (Summer 1969), 187-90.

McConnell, Virginia. "Alan Swallow and Western Writers." *South Dakota Review,* V (Summer 1967), 88-97.

Manfred, Frederick. "Alan Swallow: Poet and Publisher." *The Denver Quarterly,* II (Spring 1967), 27-31.

North, Dennis D. "Alan Swallow: A Bibliographical Checklist." *The Denver Quarterly,* II (Spring 1967), 63-72.

Ross, Morton L. "Alan Swallow and Modern, Western American Poetry." *Western American Literature,* I (Summer 1966), 97-104.

Waters, Frank. "Notes on Alan Swallow." *The Denver Quarterly,* II (Spring 1967), 16-25.

Winters, Yvor. "Alan Swallow: 1915-1966." *The Southern Review,* III (July 1967), 796-8.

JOHN SWETT

Polos, Nicholas C. "Early California Poetry." *The California Historical Society Quarterly,* XLVIII (September 1969), 243-55.

BELLA FRENCH SWISHER

Dickey, Imogene. "Bella French Swisher: Texas Editor and Litterateur." *Southwestern American Literature,* I (January 1971), 8-11.

BAYARD TAYLOR

Doughty, Nanelia S. "Bayard Taylor: First California Booster." *Western Review,* VII (Spring 1970), 22-7.

Doughty, Nanelia S. "Bayard Taylor's Second Look at California (1859)." *Western Review,* VIII (Winter 1971), 51-5.

JOHN WILLIAM THOMASON, JR.

Dykes, Jeff C. "Tentative Bibliographic Check Lists of Western Illustrators: XXXV, John William Thomason, Jr. (1893-1944)." *American Book Collector,* XVII (April 1967), 17-20.

Graves, John. "The Old Breed: A Note on John W. Thomason, Jr."
Southwest Review, LIV (Winter 1969), 36-46.

Norwood, W. D. *John W. Thomason, Jr.* Southwest Writers Series,
No. 25. Austin, Texas: Steck-Vaughn Company, 1969.

Perkins, Maxwell. *Editor to Author.* New York: Charles Scribner's
Sons, 1950. Contains letters to and about Thomason.

Willock, Roger. *Lone Star Marine: A Biography of the Late Colonel
John W. Thomason, Jr., U.S.M.C.* Princeton, N J.: Roger
Willock, 1961.

THOMAS BANGS THORPE

Blair, Walter. "Technique in 'The Big Bear of Arkansas.' " *Southwest Review*, XXVIII (1943), 426-35.

Current-Garcia, Eugene. "Thomas Bangs Thorpe and the Literature
of the Ante-Bellum Southwestern Frontier." *Louisiana Historical
Quarterly*, XXXIX (April 1956), 199-222.

Rickels, Milton. "Thomas Bangs Thorpe (1815-1878)." *A
Bibliographical Guide to the Study of Southern Literature.* Baton
Rouge: Louisiana State University Press, 1969, 308-9.

Rickels, Milton. *Thomas Bangs Thorpe: Humorist of the Old Southwest.* Baton Rouge: Louisiana State University Press, 1962.

Simoneaux, Katherine G. "Symbolism in Thorpe's 'The Big Bear of
Arkansas.' " *Arkansas Historical Quarterly*, XXV (Fall 1966),
240-7.

WALLACE THURMAN

Haslam, Gerald. "Wallace Thurman: A Western Renaissance Man."
Western American Literature, VI (Spring 1971), 53-9.

B. TRAVEN

Miller, C. H., and R. E. Pujan, eds. "B. Traven." *Texas Quarterly*, VI
(1963), 161-211.

Stone, Judy. "The Mystery of B. Traven." *Ramparts*, VI (1967), 31-
49, 55-69 ff.

Warner, John M. "Tragic Vision in B. Traven's 'The Night of the
Visitor.' " *Studies in Short Fiction*, VII (Summer 1970), 377-84.

FREDERICK JACKSON TURNER

Boyle, Thomas E. "Frederick Jackson Turner and Thomas Wolfe: The Frontier as History and Literature." *Western American Literature*, IV (Winter 1970), 273-85.

Jacobs, Wilbur R. "The Many-Sided Frederick Jackson Turner." *The Western Historical Quarterly*, I (October 1970), 363-72.

Lewis, Merrill E. "American Frontier History as Literature: Studies in Historiography of George Bancroft, Frederick Jackson Turner, and Thoeodore Roosevelt." Unpublished doctoral dissertation, University of Utah, 1968.

Simonson, Harold P. "Frederick Jackson Turner: Frontier History as Art." *Antioch Review*, XXIV (1964), 201-11.

MARK TWAIN
See Samuel Clemens

I. L. UDELL

Jason, Rick. "Udell." *South Dakota Review*, VII (Spring 1969), 5-7.

Milton, John R. "Udell—The Taos Man." *South Dakota Review*, VII (Spring 1969), 107-23.

DAVID WAGONER

Schafer, William J. "David Wagoner's Fiction: In the Mills of Satan." *Critique*, IX (No. 1), 71-89.

STANLEY WALKER

Milner, Jay. "Stanley Walker: The Retread Texan." *The Arlington Quarterly*, II (Summer 1969), 7-21.

ARTEMAS WARD
See Charles Farrar Brown

EUGENE FITCH WARE

Malin, James C. "The Burlington, Iowa, Apprenticeship of the Kansas Poet Eugene Fitch Ware, 'Ironquill.' " *Iowa Journal of History*, LVII (July 1959), 193-230.

Malin, James C. "Eugene F. Ware, Master Poet." *Kansas Historical Quarterly*, XXXII (1967), 401-25.

Malin, James C. "Notes on the Poetic Debts of Eugene F. Ware—Ironquil." *The Kansas Historical Quarterly*, XXXV (Summer 1969), 165-81.

FRANK WATERS

Bucco, Martin. *Frank Waters.* Southwest Writers Series, No. 22. Austin, Texas: Steck-Vaughn Company, 1969.

Huntress, Diana. "The Man Who Resurrected the Deer." *South Dakota Review*, VI (Winter 1968-69), 69-71.

Lyon, Thomas J. "An Ignored Meaning of the West." *Western American Literature*, III (Spring 1968), 51-9.

Milton, John R. "Conversation with Frank Waters." *South Dakota Review*, IX (Spring 1971), 16-27.

Milton, John R. "The Land as Form in Frank Waters and William Eastlake." *Kansas Quarterly*, II (Spring 1970), 104-9.

Pilkington, William T. "Character and Landscape: Frank Waters' Colorado Trilogy." *Western American Literature*, II (Fall 1967), 183-93.

Waters, Frank, ed. "Bibliography of the Works of Frank Waters." *South Dakota Review*, IV (Summer 1966), 77-8.

Young, Vernon. "Frank Waters: Problems of the Regional Imperative." *New Mexico Quarterly Review*, XIX (1949), 353-72.

NATHANIEL WEST

Light, James F. *Nathaniel West: An Interpretive Study.* 2nd ed. Evanston: Northwestern University Press, 1971.

Reid, Randall. *The Fiction of Nathaniel West: No Redeemer, No Promised Land.* Chicago: University of Chicago Press, 1971.

Scott, Nathan A., Jr. *Nathaniel West: A Critical Essay.* Grand Rapids: Eerdmans, 1971.

White, William. "Nathaniel West: A Bibliography." *Studies in Bibliography*, XI (1958), 207-24.

STEWART EDWARD WHITE

Butte, Edna Rosemary. "Stewart Edward White: His Life and Literary Career." Unpublished doctoral dissertation, University of Southern California, 1960.

Jones, Howard Mumford. *The Age of Energy: Varieties of American Experience, 1865-1915.* New York: The Viking Press, 1971, 303-6.

Saxton, Eugene F. *Stewart Edward White.* New York: Doubleday, Page and Company, n.d.

Underwood, John Curtis. "Stewart Edward White and All Outdoors." *Literature and Insurgency: Ten Studies in Racial Evolution.* New York: Mitchell Kennerley 1914, 254-98.

WILLIAM ALLEN WHITE

Groman, George L. "The Political Fiction of William Allen White: A Study in Emerging Progressivism." *The Midwest Quarterly,* VIII (October 1966), 79-93.

OPAL WHITELEY

Bede, Elbert. *Fabulous Opal Whiteley: From Logging Camp to Princess of India.* Portland: Binfords and Mort, 1954.

Holbrook, Stewart H. *Far Corner: A Personal View of the Pacific Northwest.* New York: The Macmillan Company, 1952, 209-19.

WALT WHITMAN

Allen, Gay Wilson. *Walt Whitman Handbook.* New York, 1946.

Allen, Gay Wilson. *The Solitary Singer: A Critical Biography of Walt Whitman.* New York, 1955.

Bulow, Ernest. "The Poet of the West: Walt Whitman and the Native American Voice." *The Possible Sack* [University of Utah], III (November 1971), 7-10.

Canby, Henry Seidel. *Walt Whitman: An American.* Boston: Houghton Mifflin Company, 1943.

Coffman, S. K., Jr. "Form and Meaning in Whitman's 'Passage to India.'" *PMLA,* LXX (June 1955), 337-49.

Fussell, Edwin. *Frontier: American Literature and the American West.* Princeton University Press, 1965, 397-441.

Hubach, Robert R. "Walt Whitman and the West." Unpublished doctoral dissertation, Indiana University, 1943.

Huffstickler, Star. "Walt Whitman as a Precursor of Frederick Jackson Turner." *Walt Whitman Review*, VIII (March 1962), 3-8.

Lovell, John Jr. "Appreciating Whitman: 'Passage to India.'" *Modern Language Quarterly*, XXI (June 1960), 131-41.

Miller, James E., Jr. *A Critical Guide to Leaves of Grass*. Chicago, 1957.

Nelson, Herbert B. "Walt Whitman and the Westward Movement." Unpublished doctoral dissertation, University of Washington, 1945.

Smith, Henry Nash. *Virgin Land: The American West as Symbol and Myth*. New York: Vintage Books, n.d., 47-51.

Steensma, Robert C. "Whitman and General Custer." *Walt Whitman Review*, X (June 1964), 41-2.

Thorp, Willard. "Whitman." *Eight American Authors*, ed. Floyd Stovall. New York: W. W. Norton and Company, 1963, 271-318, 445-51.

HERBERT WILNER

Wilner, Herbert. "Dovisch: Things, Facts, and Rainbows." in Ray B. West, Jr. *The Art of Writing Fiction*. New York: Thomas Y. Crowell Company, 1968, 110-6.

YVOR WINTERS

Abood, Edward. "Some Observations on Yvor Winters." *Chicago Review*, XI (Autumn 1957), 51-66.

Holloway, John. "The Critical Theory of Yvor Winters." *Critical Quarterly*, VII (Spring 1965), 54-66.

Lohf, Kenneth A., and E. P. Sheehy. "Yvor Winters: A Bibliography." *Twentieth Century Literature*, V (April 1959), 27-51.

Marsh, Robert. "Observations on the Criticism of Yvor Winters." *Spectrum*, IV (Fall 1960), 146-62.

Pearson, Gabriel. "The Defeat of Yvor Winters." *Review*, VIII (August 1963), 3-12.

Ramsey, Paul. "Yvor Winters: Some Abstractions Against Abstraction." *Sewanee Review*, LXXIII (Summer 1965), 451-64.

Sexton, Richard J. "The Complex of Yvor Winters Criticism." Unpublished doctoral dissertation, Fordham University, 1965.

Stephens, Alan. "The Collected Poems of Yvor Winters." *Twentieth Century Literature,* IX (1963), 127-39.
Van Deusen, Marshall. "In Defense of Yvor Winters." *Thought,* XXXII (Autumn 1957), 409-36.

SOPHUS K. WINTHER

Meldrum, Barbara. "Structure and Meaning in S. K. Winther's *Beyond the Garden Gate." Western American Literature,* VI (Fall 1971), 191-202.
Powell, Desmond. "Sophus Winther: The Grimsen Trilogy." *American Scandinavian Review,* XXXVI (June 1948), 144-7.
Quinn, Arthur Hobson, ed. *The Literature of the American People.* New York: Appleton-Century-Crofts, 1951, 912-3.
Whicher, George F. "Dane in America." *Forum,* CVI (November 1946), 450-4.

OWEN WISTER

Agnew, S. M. "Destry Goes on Riding: *The Virginian." Publisher's Weekly,* CLVII (August 23, 1952, 746-51.
Baldwin, Charles C. "Owen Wister." *The Men Who Make Our Novels.* New York: Dodd, Mead, 1925, 590-600.
Barsness, John A. "Theodore Roosevelt as Cowboy: The Virginian as Jacksonian Man." *American Quarterly,* XXI (Fall 1969), 609-19.
Bechard, Eugene Earsel. "Social Criticism in the Novels and Short Stories of Owen Wister." Unpublished master's thesis, Washington State College, 1953.
Boatright, Mody C. "The American Myth Rides the Range: Owen Wister's Man on Horseback." *Southwest Review,* XXXVI (Summer 1951), 157-63.
Bode, Carl. "Henry James and Owen Wister." *American Literature,* XXVI (May 1954), 250-2.
Branch, Douglas. *The Cowboy and His Interpreters.* New York: D. Appleton and Company, 1926.
Bratcher, James T. "Owen Wister's *The Virginian:* Two Corrections." *Western Folklore,* XXI (1962), 188-90.
Cooper, Frederic Taber. "Owen Wister." *Some American Story Tellers.* New York: Henry Holt and Company, 1911, 265-94.
Durham, Philip. "Introduction:" and "Textual Note." *The Virginian: A Horeseman of the Plains,* by Owen Wister. Riverside Edition. Boston: Houghton Mifflin Company, 1968.

Fiske, Horace Spencer. *Provincial Types in American Fiction.* Chautauqua, New York: Chautauqua Press, 1903, 215-40.

Frantz, Joe B., and Julian Ernest Choate, Jr. *The American Cowboy: The Myth and the Reality.* Norman: University of Oklahoma Press, 1955.

Gemme, Francis R. *Wister's The Virginian.* Monarch Notes and Study Guides. New York: Thor Publications, 1966.

Houghton, Donald E. "Two Heroes in One: Reflections Upon the Popularity of *The Virginian." Journal of Popular Culture,* IV (Fall 1970), 497-506.

Hubbell, Jay B. "Owen Wister's Work." *South Atlantic Quarterly,* XXIX (1930), 440-3.

Lambert, Neal. "Owen Wister—The 'Real Incident' and the 'Thrilling Story.' " *The American West: An Appraisal,* ed. Robert G. Ferris. Santa Fe: Museum of New Mexico Press, 1963, 191-200.

Lambert, Neal. "Owen Wister's 'Hank's Woman': The Writer and His Comment." *Western American Literature,* IV (Spring 1969), 39-50.

Lambert, Neal. "Owen Wister's Lin McLean: The Failure of the Vernacular Hero." *Western American Literature,* V (Fall 1970), 219-32.

Lambert, Neal. Owen Wister's Virginian: The Genesis of a Cultural Hero." *Western American Literature,* VI (Summer 1971), 99-107.

Lambert, Neal. "The Values of the Frontier: Owen Wister's Final Assessment." *South Dakota Review,* IX (Spring 1971), 76-87.

Lambert, Neal Elwood. "The Western Writing of Owen Wister: The Conflict of East and West." Unpublished doctoral dissertation, University of Utah, 1966.

Lewis, Marvin. "Owen Wister: Caste Imprints in Western Letters." *Arizona Quarterly,* X (Summer 1954), 147-56.

Mason, Julian. "Owen Wister, Boy Librarian." *The Quarterly Journal of the Library of Congress,* XXVI (October 1969), 201-12.

[Mayfield, John S.] "A Note about Owen Wister." *The Courier* [Syracuse University Library], XXVI (1966), 29-36.

Rush, N. Orwin. "Frederic Remington and Owen Wister: The Story of Friendship," in K. Ross Toole *et al.,* eds., *Probing the American West.* Santa Fe: Museum of New Mexico Press, 1962, 154-7.

Stokes, Frances Kemble Wister. *My Father, Owen Wister, and Ten Letters Written by Owen Wister to his Mother during his First Trip to Wyoming in 1885.* Laramie: University of Wyoming Library Associates, 1952.

Trombley, W. "Another Western: Owen Wister's Virginian." *Saturday Evening Post,* CCXXXIV (December 23, 1961), 98-101.

Vorpahl, Ben M. "Ernest Hemingway and Owen Wister." *Library Chronicle*, XXXVI (Spring 1970), 126-37.

Vorpahl, Ben M. "Henry James and Owen Wister." *The Pennsylvania Magazine of History and Biography*, XCV (July 1971), 291-338.

Vorpahl, Ben M. "Very Much Like a Firecracker: Owen Wister on Mark Twain." *Western American Literature*, VI (Summer 1971), 83-98.

Walbridge, Earle F. *"The Virginian* and Owen Wister: A Bibliography." *The Papers of the Bibliographical Society of America*, XLVI (1952), 117-20.

Walker, Don D. "Essays in the Criticism of Western Literary Criticism: II. The Dogmas of DeVoto." *The Possible Sack* [University of Utah], III (November 1971), 1-7.

Walker, Don D. "Wister, Roosevelt and James: A Note on the Western." *American Quarterly*, XII (Fall 1960), 358-66.

Watkins, George T. "Owen Wister and The American West: A Bibliography and Critical Study." Unpublished doctoral dissertation, University of Illinois, 1959.

Watkins, George T. "Wister and 'The Virginian.' " *The Pacific Northwesterner*, II (Fall 1958), 49-52.

White, G. Edward. *The Eastern Establishment and the Western Experience: The West of Frederick Remington, Theodore Roosevelt, and Owen Wister.* New Haven: Yale University Press, 1968.

White, John I. "Owen Wister and the Dogies." *Journal of American Folklore*, LXXXII (January-March 1969), 66-9.

White, John I. "The Virginian." *Montana Magazine of Western History*, XVI (October 1966), 2-11.

Wister, Fanny K. "Letters of Owen Wister, Author of *The Virginian.*" *The Pennsylvania Magazine of History and Biography*, LXXXIII (January 1959), 3-28.

Wister, Fanny Kemble. "Owen Wister Out West." *Midway*, X (April 1962), 24-49.

Wister, Fanny Kemble. "Owen Wister's West." *Atlantic Monthly*, CXCV (May 1955), 29-35; (June 1955), 52-7.

Wister, Owen. *Owen Wister Out West: His Journals and Letters*, ed. Fanny Kemble Wister. Chicago: University of Chicago Press, 1958.

Wister, Owen. "Strictly Hereditary." *Musical Quarterly*, XXII (January 1936), 1-7.

Wister, Owen. *The Virginian.* New York: Washington Square Press, 1964. This edition includes helpful editorial materials.

Wister, Owen. *The Virginian.* Introductions by Sidney C. Clark. New York: Airmont Publishing Co., 1964. Edition includes helpful introduction.

THOMAS WOLFE

Boyle, Thomas E. "Frederick Jackson Turner and Thomas Wolfe: The Frontier as History and Myth." *Western American Literature*, IV (Winter 1970), 273-85.

Chittick, V. L. O. "Thomas Wolfe's Farthest West." *Southwest Review*, XLVIII (Spring 1963), 93-110.

Cracroft, Richard H. "Through Utah and the Western Parks: Thomas Wolfe's Farewell to America." *Utah Historical Quarterly*, XXXVII (Summer 1969), 291-306.

Powell, Desmond. "Of Thomas Wolfe." *Arizona Quarterly*, I (Spring 1945), 28-36.

Wolfe, Thomas. *A Western Journal*. Pittsburgh: University of Pittsburgh Press, 1951. Includes a helpful introductory note by Edward Aswell.

CHARLES ERSKINE SCOTT WOOD

Bingham, Edwin. "Oregon's Romantic Rebels: John Reed and Charles Erskine Scott Wood." *Pacific Northwest Quarterly*, L (July 1959).

HAROLD BELL WRIGHT

Gaston, Edwin W., Jr. *The Early Novel of the Southwest*. Albuquerque: University of New Mexico Press, 1961.